Country Style
Painted Wood Projects

Country Style Painted Wood Projects

by **Primrose Path**

with Donna Kooler Design Studio

Sterling Publishing Co., Inc. New York

A Sterling/Chapelle Book

Designs:

John and Linda Alexander
Lorna McRoden

Instructions:

Linda Alexander
Lorna McRoden

Kooler Design Studio, Inc.:

President: Donna Kooler

Executive Vice President:
 Linda Gillum

Editors: Loretta Heden
 Deanna Hall West

Chapelle Ltd.:

Owner: Jo Packham

Editor: Amanda Beth McPeck

Staff: Malissa Boatwright
 Sara Casperson
 Rebecca Christensen
 Amber Hansen
 Holly Hollingsworth
 Susan Jorgensen
 Susan Laws
 Barbara Milburn
 Pat Pearson
 Leslie Ridenour
 Cindy Rooks
 Cindy Stoeckl
 Ryanne Webster
 Nancy Whitley

Photography: Kevin Dilley for
 Hazen Photography

Photography Styling: Jo Packham

Photographs in this book were taken at Secret Haven, Layton, UT. Their cooperation and trust are deeply appreciated.

If you have any questions or comments or would like information on specialty products featured in this book, please contact:

Chapelle Ltd., Inc.
PO Box 9252
Ogden, UT 84409

(801) 621-2777
(801) 621-2788 (fax)

Many of the wood items in this book are available as kits from:

Primrose Path
c/o Chapelle Ltd., Inc.
PO Box 9252
Ogden, UT 84409

(801) 621-2777
(801) 621-2788 (fax)

Dedication

In loving memory to our dad, Paul Morley. He taught us to enjoy whatever work we chose to do and that having fun would ensure a job well done.
 —Linda Alexander and Lorna McRoden

With special thanks to Donna Kooler, Loretta Heden, and Deanna Hall West at Kooler Design Studio, without whose help and hard work this book would never have been accomplished.

Library of Congress Cataloging-in-Publication Data Available

Country-style painted wood projects / by Primrose Path with Donna Kooler Design Studio.
    p.   cm.
    "A Sterling/Chapelle book."
    Includes index.
    ISBN 0-8069-3150-7
    1. Painting. 2. Painted woodwork. 3. House furnishings.
  I. Primrose Path (Firm) II. Kooler Design Studio
  TT385.C69   1996
  745.7'23–dc20   96-3958
                                       CIP

10 9 8 7 6 5 4 3 2 1

Published by Sterling Publishing Company, Inc., 387 Park Avenue South, New York,
 N.Y. 10016
© 1996 by Chapelle Limited
Distributed in Canada by Sterling Publishing
c/o Canadian Manda Group, One Atlantic Avenue, Suite 105, Toronto, Ontario,
 Canada M6K 3E7
Distributed in Great Britain and Europe by Cassell PLC, Wellington House, 125 Strand,
 London WC2R OBB, England
Distributed in Australia by Capricorn Link (Australia) Pty Ltd., P.O. Box 6651,
 Baulkham Hills, Business Centre, NSW 2153, Australia
Printed in Hong Kong

Sterling ISBN 0-8069-3150-7

John & Linda Alexander
& Lorna McRoden
designers

My twin sister, Linda, and I have been designing, making crafts, and painting since we were children. We decided to really put our hearts and souls into this very exciting career nine years ago.

We began with so many ideas that we had to ask John, Linda's husband, to lend a hand. He is able to cut out the wood pieces we ask for and also come up with great ideas of his own.

The three of us started painting and wood-cutting in our homes, but have bought a hundred-year-old farmhouse in Placerville, California, where we hope to stretch and grow a bit. We have named our little farmhouse "Primrose Path."

Linda and I have had so much fun trying out new ideas that every time she and I skip hand in hand down a new primrose path, we tell John, "Come along, this will be fun!" He is always there to say, "Oh no, you'd better not go down that path, you might get into trouble!" He sounds just like Eeyore of Pooh Bear fame. Sometimes John is right, sometimes not, but, in any case, we are a team of three, each one having his or her own specialty. Linda paints beautifully, John is a wonderful woodcutter, and I do much of the drawing for our designs.

Our children (six in all) have supported our efforts and are always enthusiastic about all those Christmas gifts! They are Gayle Alexander, Michael Alexander, Janet Chapan, Rick Alexander, Jeannie Ottoveggio, and Paul Alexander. They have also blessed us with six very beautiful grandchildren.

We are so pleased to be able to present this book, hoping that others may have as much enjoyment from painting as we do.

—Lorna McRoden

Lorna McRoden (seated), Linda and John Alexander (standing)

table of contents

g e n e r a l
instructions

Wood Preparation

These first steps will make all the difference in the world in creating a beautifully finished piece.

Start by filling any small cracks or nail holes in the wood with a good wood filler. Let dry. Using a fine-grit sandpaper (180–220), sand all surfaces of the item. Sand with the grain of the wood until it has a smooth surface that feels like an eggshell to the touch. Don't forget the edges! Remove sanding dust with a tack cloth.

Sealing the Wood

Method One

For sealing and staining. Using a disposable sponge brush, apply a stain controller/wood sealer to the item. Use a sealer that is clear and will penetrate the wood so that it seals the item. Remember to sand lightly when dry, removing the "furrys" that the sealer raises. After sanding, use a tack cloth to remove any sanding dust left behind. The item is now ready for staining.

Method Two

For a washed or painted background. Apply a mixture of ⅓ water-based sealer, ⅓ acrylic paint, and ⅓ water with a disposable sponge brush. This method is used to cover the item with a "wash" or a transparent coat of color, with the grain of the wood showing (usually two coats). It can be made more opaque by applying more coats of this sealing mixture. Remember to paint the back side of the item for a more professional look. Let each coat dry before painting the second coat or transferring pattern.

Backgrounds

Stained

To stain an item, use a disposable sponge brush and wood stain. Wipe the excess stain away with a piece of cheesecloth before the stain dries. Remember to stain the back side of the item for a more professional look. Let dry thoroughly before transferring pattern.

Spattered

Use an old toothbrush (one that is used and fuzzy) for spattering. Dip toothbrush into a mixture of paint and water. Tap to remove excess paint. With the bristles pointing at the area to be spattered, brush a finger or a craft stick across the bristles. Test this method first on a piece of paper. If the mixture is too thin, it makes large spots instead of spatters. After spattering the item, let it dry before transferring pattern.

Transferring the Pattern

Trace pattern from the line drawing onto a sheet of tracing paper. Place traced pattern onto wood item and secure one edge with a piece of transparent tape. Slip a piece of transfer paper, transfer side down, between wood and tracing. Trace over design using a stylus or an inkless ballpoint pen. Use a light touch, because pressing too hard can dent the wood or make marks that are too hard to cover. Lift off tracing and transfer paper.

Base Coating

The first color applied to a design area is the base coat. Use a round or flat brush to fill in the areas of the design. Apply a smooth coat of paint mixed with a bit of water to the designated area. Leave a fine line between color areas. Usually two coats will be needed to cover an area, but be sure to let each coat dry before adding another or the paint will "lift" off. All areas of design should be base-coated before adding shading or highlighting.

Paper Sanding

Paper-sand between coats to keep area smooth. Simply rub or sand the item with a piece of brown paper grocery bag.

Side Loading

For shading and highlighting. Dress a flat brush with either a flow medium or water (either one works well). To dress brush, dip it into medium, then lay it on a paper towel until excess liquid disappears.

Dip the corner of one side of brush into paint. Blend paint into brush by brushing it back and forth in the same spot on a paper palette, letting the intensity of the color move across the brush, blending it gradually from dark, to medium, to light, to nothing. Apply color to shaded or highlighted area of work. This technique sounds difficult, but once mastered, it is really the most fun part of painting. It is used for most of the projects in this book.

A halo of color can occur when side loading. It is caused by over-blending and allowing the paint to travel entirely across the brush. When this happens, rinse brush and reload, or pinch brush between thumb and forefinger, on the opposite side from the loaded paint, to squeeze out excess liquid. Test this side-loading technique before painting an item.

Line Work

For accents, outlines, and single-line details. Thin paint with water or flow medium. Paint should be the consistency of light cream or ink, and should flow from the brush like ink flows from a pen.

Using a good script liner brush, load the thinned paint all the way from the tip to the ferrule (metal ring). To load the liner brush, lay it in a puddle of thinned paint, and pull the brush towards yourself while rotating it. Touch the tip of the brush to the palette to remove the tiny drop of paint at the end of the bristles.

When lining, use just the tip of the brush. Use a light pressure for thin lines and a heavier pressure for the thicker lines. Be sure to use your wrist, not just your fingers, while pulling out the line in a smooth motion.

Layering

For a blended oil-painted look that adds dimension. Also called the dab, pat, and blend method.
❶ Transfer design to painted or stained background of item.
❷ Using a soft brush (round or flat), mix a dab of paint and water (in small equal proportions) on a paper palette. Water, which is a flow medium, will keep the acrylic paint wet so there will be time to dab, pat, and blend.
❸ Dab or pat the paint mixture onto the appropriate area, starting in the center and gradually moving to the outside edges of the area, creating a soft or feathered edge.
❹ Each layer is comprised of one color. This is the way to build the layers.
❺ The last layer usually includes any fine line work called for on the design.
❻ Build the layers in this way, letting each layer dry before preceding to the next. If it isn't dry, the color will "lift" off.

Finishing

This last step is as important as the first steps.

Use a damp cotton swab to rub off any transfer lines that are not covered with paint.

Use a good water-based varnish and a good-quality glaze brush. If a good brush isn't used, bubbles will form on the surface of the item. Lay the varnish down with long even strokes,

changing the direction of the strokes with each coat. Apply several coats, particularly if the item is to be used outdoors. Let each coat dry separately.

A clear matte spray acrylic finish can also be used. Spray on several light coats, letting each coat dry separately.

Tips and Tricks

Hearts and Dots

Use the round handle end of a paintbrush or a wood dowel, and dip the end into a puddle of paint, one dip per dot.

For hearts, place two dots side by side. With a stylus or round brush handle, pull the wet dots down into a "V," letting the paint fill into the bottom of the heart.

The size of the dots or hearts depends on the size of the handle end or dowel used.

Back to Front

Always work from the background of the design to the front. For instance, lay down tendrils or line work first, then do the basic leaf color, then shade and highlight the leaves. Next, paint the rose or rosebud, and finish with the hearts or dots, because these take the longest to dry.

Brush Cleaning

Remember to keep brushes clean between painting sessions. Use a brush cleaner or soft soap to clean out excess paint, rinse,

and shape for the next use. Brushes are expensive, but they will last a long time if taken care of properly.

A good trick for removing dried paint is to soak the brush in rubbing alcohol for a few hours, then rinse and clean as usual.

Splashes

If paint splashes or drips onto the item, don't panic. Keep a small bottle of rubbing alcohol near the work area, along with some cotton swabs. Dip the swab into the alcohol and then dab gently at the spot until it is removed. This method is a great way to get the paint spots out of clothes as well.

Shaping Brushes

You can shape brushes after use with dish soap. Make sure to thoroughly rinse brush before next use.

Handle Ends of Brushes

The handle end of a brush is often used to create dots and dot hearts. You can create the perfect size for your dots if you sharpen the end in a pencil sharpener (the handle must be wooden to do this). This technique is especially good for old brushes that seem to have lost their usefulness.

general Supplies

Tools and Materials

Adhesive/sealant
All-purpose water-base sealer
Brown paper grocery bag
Brush basin
Brush cleaner
Clear matte spray acrylic finish
Cotton swabs
Drill and bit set
Fine-grit sandpaper (180–220)
Fine-line black marker
Fine-line ink pen
Flow medium
Hammer
Hot glue gun and glue
Needle-nose pliers
Oak-colored wood stain
Old toothbrush
Paint brushes
   Flats: #2, 4, 6, 8, 10, 12
   Rounds: #001, 1, 2, 3
   Script liners: #10/0, 1, 2
   Glaze brush: ¾" wide
   Sponge brushes: 1" and 2"
    wide
Paper palette or plate
Paper towels or cheesecloth
Rubbing alcohol
Ruler
Scroll saw
Sea sponge

Soft lead pencil
Stain controller/wood sealer
Stylus
Tack cloth
Toothpicks
Tracing paper
Transparent tape
Water-base varnish
White and colored transfer paper
White chalk pencil
White vinegar
Wire cutters
Wood dowels (⅛", ¼", ⁵⁄₁₆", ⅜",
   ½", ⅝", and 1" dia.)
Wood filler
Wood glue

Acrylic Paint Palette

Pinks

Pale Pink
Light Pink
Medium Pink
Dark Pink
Pink
Light Rose Pink
Dark Rose Pink

Reds

Bright Red
Cadmium Red

Napthol Crimson
Barn Red
Cranberry
Raspberry Wine
Dark Wine Red
Very Dark Red
Dark Red

Oranges/Corals

Blush
Dark Flesh
Orange
Light Peach
Medium Peach
Dark Peach
Medium Coral

Yellows/Golds

Creamy Yellow
Light Yellow
Light Butter Yellow
Butter Yellow
Golden Yellow
Medium Gold
Light Gold Metallic

Greens

Very Pale Green
Pale Green
Light Yellow-Green
Medium Yellow-Green
Dark Yellow-Green
Christmas Green
Olive Green

Teals

Pale Teal
Medium Teal
Teal Green
Medium Dark Teal

Blues

Pale Blue
Soft Light Blue
Medium Light Blue
Medium Blue
Medium Dark Blue
Dark Blue
Light Gray-Blue
Medium Gray-Blue
Dark Gray-Blue
Dark Blue-Gray

Purples

Light Periwinkle Blue
Lilac
Light Violet
Light Violet-Blue
Violet-Blue
Light Purple
Dark Purple

Tans/Browns

Light Tan
Dark Tan
Medium Brown
Medium Yellow-Brown
Chocolate Brown

Grays/Blacks

Dove Gray
Charcoal
Very Dark Gray
Black

Whites

Pure White
Soft White

w a r t t h e
f r o g

Designed by Lorna McRoden

Little Wart is a true prince among frogs.

Read General Instructions before beginning any project. Trace Wart the Frog patterns on pg. 16 onto tracing paper, omitting slash marks which indicate shaded areas.

Specific Materials Needed

9" x 10" of ¾"-thick clear pine (front and back)
Wood bell handle with hole near top (1" high)
Wood button (1½" dia.)
Wood heart (¾" wide x ¼" thick)
Wood heart spacer (1" wide x ½" thick)
Scroll saw
Drill and ⅛"-dia. bit
All-purpose water-base sealer
Stylus
Colored transfer paper
Disposable sponge brush (1" wide)
18" of ¼"-wide orchid satin ribbon
Black fine-line marker pen
Flat brush (#8 and #12)
Script liner brush (#10/0)
Round brush (#2)
Clear matte spray acrylic finish
Adhesive/sealant

Acrylic Paint Palette

Light Rose Pink
Creamy Yellow
Golden Yellow
Pale Green
Dark Yellow-Green
Medium Dark Teal
Medium Blue
Black
Soft White

Preparation

❶ Using pattern and scroll saw, cut out Front and Back.
❷ If bell handle does not have a hole, drill one using ⅛"-dia. bit.
❸ Prepare wood for painting, referring to Wood Preparation on pg. 8.
❹ Using disposable sponge brush, wash all sides of Front, Back, and spacer with a mixture of ⅓ Pale Green paint, ⅓ water, and ⅓ all-purpose water-base sealer. Usually two coats are needed. Let each coat dry separately. Lightly paper-sand after each coat.
❺ Match traced outline of Front and Back designs with wood pieces. Using stylus and transfer paper, trace designs.

When painting dimensional items, paint one side and edges; let dry. Paint remaining side. Refer to Colored Example on pg. 15, patterns, and photo for shading and details.

Eyes

❶ Using round brush and Creamy Yellow paint, base-paint lower half of each eye using two coats.
❷ Using round brush and Black paint, base-paint upper part of each eye. Let dry.

Shading

Use #8 flat brush side loaded with paint. Refer to slash marks on patterns for placement.
❶ Using Golden Yellow paint, shade bottom edge of lower part of each eye.
❷ Using Dark Yellow-Green paint, shade Back.
❸ Using Dark Yellow-Green paint, shade under mouth, behind eye ridges, along shoulders, and between toes on Front.

Highlight

Using #8 flat brush side loaded with Soft White paint, highlight above upper lip and along top edge of eye ridges.

Lining

Refer to patterns for placement and to Tips and Tricks on pg. 9 before beginning.
❶ Using script liner brush and Medium Dark Teal paint, line along shaded areas of Back piece. Line mouth, cheeks, eye ridges, and between toes on Front piece.
❷ Using script liner brush and Black paint, line around yellow part of eyes.

Details

❶ Using stylus and Medium Dark Teal paint, place a dot at end of each eye ridge and at ends of mouth line.
❷ Using stylus and Soft White paint, place two dots at top of each pupil.

Pacifier

Use #12 flat brush.
❶ Using Medium Blue paint, base-paint all sides of bell handle and wood button.
❷ Using Light Rose Pink paint, base-paint all sides of wood heart.
❸ Match traced outline of Lettering pattern with heart. Using stylus and transfer paper, trace lettering.

❹ Using Black marker, line and dot lettering.

Use adhesive/sealant to assemble.

❶ Use a damp cotton swab to remove remaining transfer lines.
❷ Spray all sides of wood items with matte spray acrylic finish. Apply three coats.
❸ Center and glue heart spacer to center back of Front piece. Center and glue back of Front piece over front of Back piece. Let dry.
❹ To create pacifier, glue base of bell handle to one side of button. Glue heart to other side of button.
❺ Slip ribbon through hole in handle of pacifier. Use an overhand knot to tie ends together. Drape pacifier over head.

Additional Ideas

❤ Paint three frogs different whimsical colors. When they sit together on a shelf, they brighten up any room.

❤ Write a birthday child's name on the heart pacifier.

❤ Paint several frogs different colors, one for each holiday, and hang appropriate pacifiers from their necks.

flopsie rabbit

Designed by Lorna McRoden

Flopsie has a carrot pacifier. Read General Instructions before beginning any project. Trace Flopsie Rabbit patterns on pg. 16 onto tracing paper, omitting slash marks which indicate shaded areas.

Specific Materials Needed

9" x 10" of ¾"-thick clear pine (Front and Back)
Wood bell handle with hole near top (1" high)
Wood button (1½" dia.)
Wood flag tip or another similarly shaped wood piece (1¼" high, carrot)
Wood heart spacer (1" wide x ½" thick)
Scroll saw
Drill and ⅛"-dia. bit
All-purpose water-base sealer
Stylus
Colored transfer paper
Disposable sponge brush (1" wide)
18" of ¼"-wide yellow satin ribbon
Flat brush (#8)
Script liner brush (#10/0)
Round brush (#2)
Clear matte spray acrylic finish
Adhesive/sealant

Acrylic Paint Palette

Dark Pink
Light Rose Pink
Orange
Medium Yellow-Green
Medium Gray-Blue
Light Tan
Medium Yellow-Brown
Dove Gray
Black
Soft White

Preparation

❶ Using pattern and scroll saw, cut out Front and Back.
❷ If bell handle does not have a hole, drill one using ⅛"-dia. bit.
❸ Prepare wood for painting, referring to Wood Preparation on pg. 8.
❹ Using disposable sponge brush, wash all sides of Front, Back, and spacer with a mixture of ⅓ Soft White paint, ⅓ water, and ⅓ all-purpose water-base sealer. Usually two coats are needed. Let each coat dry separately. Lightly paper-sand after each coat.
❺ Match traced outline of Front and Back designs with wood

pieces. Using stylus and transfer paper, trace designs.

When painting dimensional items, paint one side and edges; let dry. Paint remaining side. Refer to patterns and photo for shading and details.

Base Coating

Use round brush and two coats for base painting.

❶ Using Light Tan paint, paint lower part of eyes.
❷ Using Black paint, paint upper part of eyes.
❸ Using Light Rose Pink paint, paint nose and inside of ears.
❹ Using Medium Yellow-Green paint, paint bell handle and wood button.
❺ Using Orange paint, paint carrot (flag tip).

Shading

Use #8 flat brush side loaded with paint. Refer to slash marks on patterns for placement.

❶ Using Dove Gray paint, shade Back piece. Shade inside edge of each eye, below mouth, between and below ears, shoulder, and between toes on Front piece.

❷ Using Medium Yellow-Brown paint, shade bottom edge of lower part of eyes.

❸ Using Dark Pink paint, shade inside of ears.

❹ Using Light Rose Pink paint, shade across top of nose.

Lining

Refer to patterns for placement and to Tips and Tricks on pg. 9 before beginning.

❶ Using script liner brush and Medium Gray-Blue paint, line along shaded areas of Back piece. Line eyelashes, mouth, along top of head, between ears, along shoulders, and between toes on Front piece.

❷ Using script liner brush and Soft White paint, line whiskers.

Details

❶ Using stylus and Medium Gray-Blue paint, place a dot at end of each eyelash and at ends of mouth line.

❷ Using stylus and Soft White paint, place a dot at top of each pupil and at end of each whisker.

Finishing

Use adhesive/sealant to assemble.

❶ Use a damp cotton swab to remove remaining transfer lines.

❷ Spray all sides of wood items with matte spray acrylic finish. Apply three coats.

❸ Center and glue heart spacer on center back of Front piece. Center and glue back of Front piece over front of Back piece. Let dry.

❹ To create pacifier, glue base of bell handle to one side of button. Glue carrot (flag tip) to other side of button. Slip ribbon through hole in handle of pacifier. Use an overhand knot to tie ends together. Drape pacifier over head.

Additional Ideas

♥ Instead of a carrot pacifier, try an Easter egg pacifier or an egg basket for a cute holiday shelf sitter.

♥ For a gardening rabbit, hang seed packets from rabbit's neck and place her on a garden fence.

♥ For an unusual hostess' gift, hang a recipe for carrot cake from rabbit's neck.

♥ For baby's first Christmas, paint rabbit in reds and greens and hang a Christmas bell from her neck.

♥ Put a small welcome sign on Flopsie's neck and use her as a "welcome-to-the-neighborhood" gift.

This kitten has a mouse by the tail.

Read General Instructions before beginning any project. Trace Sittin' Kitten patterns on pg. 16 onto tracing paper, omitting slash marks which indicate shaded areas.

Specific Materials Needed

9" x 10" of ¾"-thick clear pine (Front and Back)
Wood bell handle with hole near top (1" high)
Wood button (1½" dia.)
Wood mouse (1½" long)
Wood heart spacer (1" wide x ½" thick)
Scroll saw
Drill and ⅛"-dia. bit
All-purpose water-base sealer
Stylus
Colored transfer paper
Disposable sponge brush (1" wide)
18" of ¼"-wide red satin ribbon
Flat brush (#8 and #12)
Script liner brush (#10/0)
Round brush (#2)
Clear matte spray acrylic finish
Adhesive/sealant

sittin' kitten

Designed by Lorna McRoden

Acrylic Paint Palette

Light Pink
Light Rose Pink
Bright Red
Light Yellow-Green
Medium Yellow-Green
Medium Gray-Blue
Dark Gray-Blue
Dove Gray
Black
Soft White
Pure White

Preparation

❶ Using pattern and scroll saw, cut out Front and Back.

❷ If bell handle does not have a hole, drill one using ⅛"-dia. bit.

❸ Prepare wood for painting, referring to Wood Preparation on pg. 8.

❹ Using a disposable sponge brush, wash all sides of head, body, and spacer with a mixture of ⅓ Dove Gray paint, ⅓ water, and ⅓ all-purpose water-base sealer. Usually two coats are needed. Let each coat dry separately. Lightly paper-sand after each coat.

⑤ Match traced outline of Front and Back designs with wood pieces. Using stylus and transfer paper, trace designs.

When painting dimensional items, paint one side and edges; let dry. Paint remaining side. Refer to patterns and photo for shading and details.

Base Coating

Use #2 round brush and two coats for base coating.
❶ Using Light Yellow-Green paint, paint lower part of each eye. Let dry.
❷ Using Light Pink paint, paint inside ears and nose.
❸ Using Black paint, paint top part of each eye.

Shading

Use #8 flat brush side loaded with paint. Refer to slash marks on patterns for placement.
❶ Using Medium Yellow-Green paint, shade bottom edge of lower part of each eye.
❷ Using Light Rose Pink paint, shade inside of ears and lower edge of nose.
❸ Using Medium Gray-Blue paint, shade remaining areas of Front and Back pieces.

Lining

Refer to patterns for placement and to Tips and Tricks on pg. 9 before beginning.
❶ Using script liner brush and Dark Gray-Blue paint, line along shaded areas of Back piece. Line eyelashes, mouth line, top of head, shoulders, and between toes on Front piece.
❷ Using fine script liner brush and Pure White paint, line whiskers and place an accent line at center top of nose.

Details

❶ Using stylus and Dark Gray-Blue paint, place a dot at end of each eyelash and at ends of mouth line.
❷ Using stylus and Soft White paint, place a dot at top of pupils.
❸ Using stylus and Pure White paint, place a dot at the end of each whisker.

Pacifier

Use #12 flat brush.
Using Bright Red paint, base-paint all sides of bell handle and wood button.

Finishing

Use adhesive/sealant to assemble.
❶ Use a damp cotton swab to remove remaining transfer lines.
❷ Spray all sides of wood items with matte spray acrylic finish. Apply three coats, letting each coat dry separately.
❸ Center and glue heart spacer to center back of Front piece. Center and glue back of Front piece over front of Back piece. Let dry.
❹ To create pacifier, glue base of bell handle to one side of button. Pull tail from mouse and glue to other side of button. Slip ribbon through hole in handle of pacifier, and use an overhand knot to tie ends together. Drape pacifier over head.

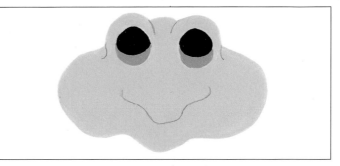

Eyes

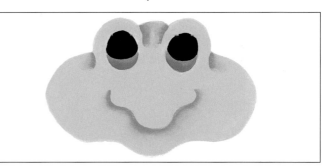

Shading

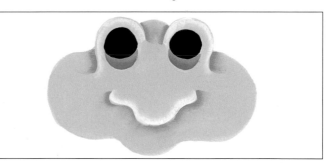

Highlight

Lining and Details
Wart the Frog Colored Example (face)

15

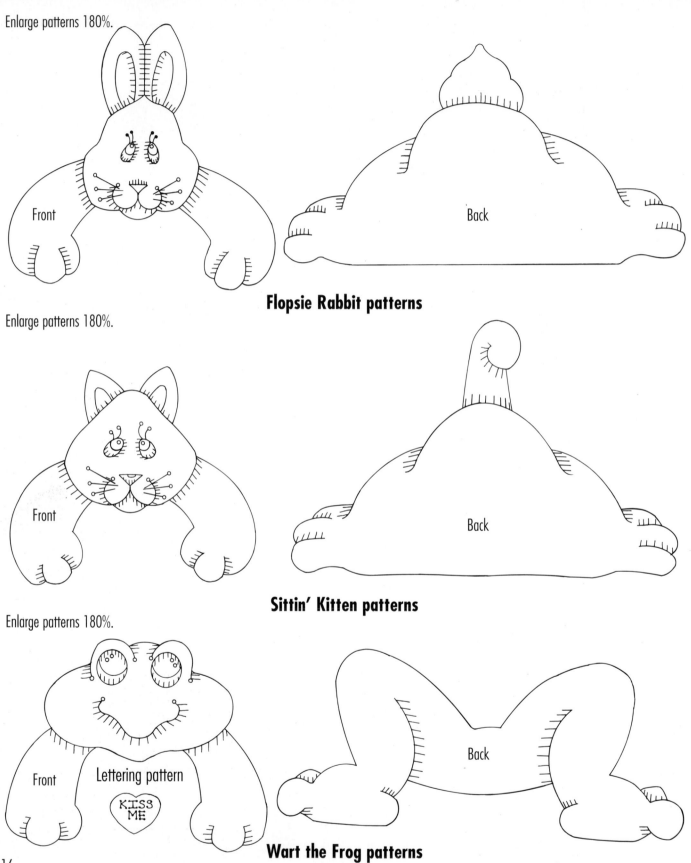

Enlarge patterns 180%.

Front

Back

Flopsie Rabbit patterns

Enlarge patterns 180%.

Front

Back

Sittin' Kitten patterns

Enlarge patterns 180%.

Front

Lettering pattern

KISS
ME

Back

Wart the Frog patterns

b a r n y a r d
Welcome

Designed by Linda Alexander

All of our animals are designed to hang from the same backboard and are interchangeable.

Read General Instructions before beginning any project. Trace Welcome and Backboard patterns on pg. 20 onto tracing paper.

4" x 12" of ¾"-thick clear pine (backboard)
3" x 11" of ½"-thick clear plywood (sign)
Band saw
Two 1½"-long drywall screws
Two ½"-dia. brass cup hooks
All-purpose water-base sealer
Disposable sponge brush (1" wide)
Colored transfer paper
Stylus
Large round-handled brush (⅜" dia.)
Small round-handled brush (⅛" dia.)
Script liner brush (#1)
Glaze brush (¾" wide)
Water-base varnish

Acrylic Paint Palette

Light Rose Pink
Medium Dark Blue
Medium Pink
Dark Blue
Medium Yellow-Green
Soft White

Preparation

❶ Using pattern and band saw, cut out backboard. Round edges. Using pattern and band saw, cut out sign.
❷ Prepare wood for painting, referring to Wood Preparation on pg. 8.
❸ Using a disposable sponge brush, wash all sides of wood items with a mixture of ⅓ Soft White paint, ⅓ water, and ⅓ all-purpose water-base sealer. Usually two coats are needed. Let each coat dry separately. Lightly paper-sand after each coat.
❹ Match traced outline of Welcome pattern with wood piece. Using stylus and transfer paper, trace design. Turn wood piece over. Retrace design onto other side of sign.
❺ Match traced outline of backboard pattern with wood piece. Using stylus and transfer paper, trace design.

When painting dimensional items, paint one side and edges; let dry. Paint remaining side. Refer to patterns and photo for placement of details.

Lining

Using script liner brush and Medium Yellow-Green paint, line decorative and scalloped lines on backboard and sign.

Lettering and Details

Read Tips and Tricks on pg. 9 before beginning steps 2–5.
❶ Using large script liner brush and Medium Dark Blue paint, line "Welcome."
❷ Using round handle of large brush and Dark Blue paint, dot ends of all letters.
❸ Using round handle of large brush and Light Rose Pink paint, make hearts to join scalloped lines at center top and bottom edges of backboard and at center top edge of sign.
❹ Using Medium Dark Blue paint, place three descending-sized dots at ends of straight lines on backboard and five descending-sized dots at ends of curved lines on sign.
❺ Using round handle of small brush and Medium Pink paint, dot points of scalloped lines on both backboard and sign.
❻ Repeat all of above steps for other side of sign.

Finishing

❶ Use a damp cotton swab to remove remaining transfer lines.
❷ Using glaze brush, apply three coats of water-based varnish to all sides of pieces. Let each coat dry separately.
❸ Using drywall screws, join backboard and sign as indicated on pattern.
❹ Attach cup hooks to bottom edge of sign 3¼" from each end.

Additional Ideas

❤ Write your name or address on the sign, and hang it next to the front door.

❤ Write the name of a birthday person on the sign, and use the sign to announce his or her party.

❤ Write "My Garden" on the sign, and hang it at your garden entrance.

h e n n y
p e n n y

Designed by Lorna McRoden

After designing and painting our animals, they invariably end up with a personality and name. This little hen looks like "Henny Penny" to us.

Read General Instructions before beginning any project. Trace Henny Penny patterns on pg. 20 onto tracing paper, omitting slash marks which indicate shaded areas.

pg. 20

Specific Materials Needed

8" sq. of ¾"-thick clear pine (body)
4" x 12" of ½"-thick clear pine (wings and feet)
Two 2" lengths of ¼"-wide brass chain
Two brass eye hooks, ¼" dia.
Scroll saw
All-purpose water-base sealer
Disposable sponge brush (1" wide)
Stylus
Colored transfer paper
Used toothbrush
Flat brush (#8)
Script liner brush (#10/0)
Round brush (#1)
Glaze brush (¾" wide)
Water-base varnish
12" of ¼"-wide yellow satin ribbon
1"-dia. brass bell
Needle-nose pliers
Adhesive/sealant

Acrylic Paint Palette

Barn Red
Dark Red
Medium Gold
Chocolate Brown
Charcoal
Black
Soft White

Preparation

❶ Using patterns and scroll saw, cut body, wings, and feet. Round edges. Wings will stand away from body if back bottom edge is beveled.
❷ Prepare wood for painting, referring to Wood Preparation on pg. 8.
❸ Using a disposable sponge brush, wash all sides of body and wings with a mixture of ⅓ Soft White paint, ⅓ water, and ⅓ all-purpose water-base sealer. Usually two coats are needed. Let each coat dry separately. Lightly paper-sand after each coat.
❹ Using a disposable sponge brush, wash all sides of feet with a mixture of ⅓ Medium Gold paint, ⅓ water, and ⅓ all-purpose water-base sealer. Usually two coats are needed. Let each coat dry separately. Lightly paper-sand after each coat.
❺ Using toothbrush and Charcoal paint, spatter-paint body and wings. Let one side dry completely before spattering other side. Refer to Backgrounds (Spattered) on pg. 8.
❻ Match traced outline of body design with wood piece. Using stylus and transfer paper, trace design onto head and tail (wing lines optional). Repeat for one wing and for feet, tracing designs onto respective wood pieces.
❼ Turn tracing paper over so that body design is reversed. Retrace head and tail designs onto other side of body. Repeat for wing design, tracing onto remaining wing piece.

When painting dimensional items, paint one side and edges; let dry. Paint remaining side. Refer to patterns and photo for placement of shading and details.

Base Coating

Use round brush.
❶ Using Medium Gold paint, paint beak with three coats. Let each coat dry separately.
❷ Using Barn Red paint, paint comb, wattle, and side of face with three coats.

Shading

Using flat brush side loaded with Dark Red paint, shade along base of comb next to head and under beak in a downward curve to separate wattle.

Lining

Use script liner brush.
❶ Using Chocolate Brown paint, line four straight lines on top side of feet and place a mouth line on beak. Carry this line across front edge to other side of hen.
❷ Using Black paint, line feathers on body and on one wing.

Details

Read Tips and Tricks in on pg. 9 before beginning.
❶ Using Medium Gold paint, place a dot for eye on one side of body. Dot should be approximately ¼" wide. Let dry.
❷ Using Black paint, place a small dot at end of all of feather lines and make a dot in center of eye slightly smaller than gold dot.
❸ Using Chocolate Brown paint, place a small dot at end of lines on feet and mouth line.

④ Using Soft White paint, place a small dot at top edge of black dot in eye. Let dry.

⑤ Repeat all of above steps for other side of hen.

Finishing

Use adhesive/sealant to assemble.

① Use a damp cotton swab to remove remaining transfer lines.

② Using glaze brush, apply three coats of water-base varnish to all sides of pieces. Let each coat dry completely.

③ Glue wings and feet to body. Refer to photo for placement.

④ Attach eye hooks to top of head and tail. Using pliers, attach a chain length to each hook. Adjust lengths as needed.

⑤ Thread bell onto ribbon. Tie ribbon around neck with a bow.

Additional Ideas

❤ Hang a wreath around Henny Penny's neck to welcome the holiday season.

❤ Change Henny Penny's look for all the seasons. Paint a raincoat for the spring, a garland of flowers for the summer, a witch's cape for the fall, and an elfin costume for the winter.

❤ For a motherly touch, glue a small wooden chick to Henny Penny's back.

Enlarge pattern 205%.

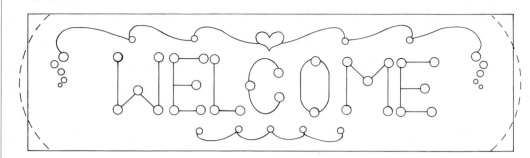

Welcome pattern

Enlarge pattern 240%.

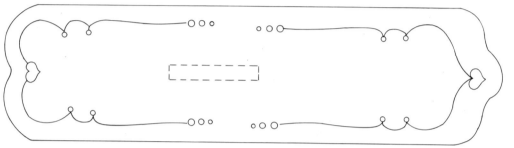

Backboard pattern

Enlarge patterns 180%.

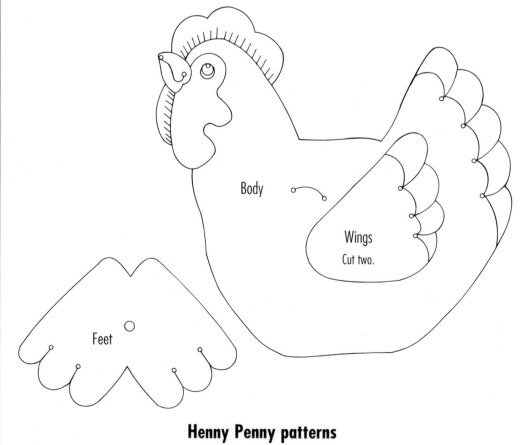

Henny Penny patterns

quacky doodle
duck

Designed by Linda Alexander

Ducks are always popular! Read General Instructions before beginning any project. Trace Quacky Doodle Duck patterns on pg. 26 onto tracing paper, omitting slash marks which indicate shaded areas.

6" x 7" of ¾"-thick clear pine (body)
5" x 12" of ½"-thick clear pine (wings and feet)
Two ¼"-dia. wood dowels (2", legs)
Two 1¼" lengths of ¼"-wide brass chain
Drill and ¼"-dia. bit
Two brass eye hooks, ¼" dia.
Scroll saw
All-purpose water-base sealer
Disposable sponge brush (1" wide)
White and colored transfer paper
Stylus
Flat brush (#8)
Script liner brush (#10/0)
Round brush (#1)
Glaze brush (¾" wide)
Water-base varnish
Needle-nose pliers
12" of ¼"-wide blue satin ribbon

1"-dia. brass bell
Adhesive/sealant

Acrylic Paint Palette

Orange
Golden Yellow
Light Gray-Blue
Dark Gray-Blue
Medium Yellow-Brown
Dove Gray
Black
Soft White
Pure White

Preparation

❶ Using patterns and scroll saw, cut wood pieces. Round edges. Wings will stand away from body if back bottom edge is beveled.
❷ Using drill and bit, drill a hole in top of each foot ¾" in from heel and ¼" deep.
❸ Find center point on bottom edge of body piece. Measure 1" to right and to left. Mark. Using drill and bit, drill two ½"-deep holes on bottom edge at marks.
❹ Prepare wood for painting, referring to Wood Preparation on pg. 8.

❺ Using a disposable sponge brush, wash all sides of duck's body and wings with a mixture of ⅓ Soft White paint, ⅓ water, and ⅓ all-purpose water-base sealer. Usually two coats are needed. Let each coat dry separately. Lightly paper-sand after each coat.
❻ Using a disposable sponge brush, wash all sides of duck's feet with a mixture of ⅓ Golden Yellow, ⅓ water, and ⅓ all-purpose water-base sealer. Usually two coats are needed. Let each coat dry separately. Lightly paper-sand after each coat.
❼ Match traced outline of body and wing design with wood pieces. Using stylus and colored transfer paper, trace designs. Turn tracing paper over so that design is reversed. Retrace design onto other side of body and other wing.
❽ Match traced outline of feet with wood piece. Using stylus and white transfer paper, trace design onto top.

When painting dimensional items, paint one side and edges; let dry. Paint remaining side. Refer to patterns and photo for placement of details.

Painting and Shading

Refer to slash marks on pattern for placement of shading.
❶ Using flat brush and Orange paint, paint legs and edges of each foot.
❷ Using flat brush side loaded with Orange paint, shade areas on feet.
❸ Using flat brush and Golden Yellow paint, base-paint bill. Carry across front edge to other side.
❹ Using flat brush side loaded with Dove Gray paint, shade next to eye and cheek.
❺ Using flat brush side loaded with Pure White paint, highlight cheek following inside of curve. Repeat when dry.

Lining

Use script liner brush.
❶ Using Medium Yellow-Brown paint, line smile. Carry line across front edge to other side of face.
❷ Using Light Gray-Blue paint, line tail and outside edge of each wing.

Details

❶ Using end of round brush and Black paint, dot eye.
❷ Using fine script liner brush and Black paint, pull out two eyelashes from eye dot.
❸ Using stylus and Black paint, dot tips of eyelashes. Let dry.
❹ Using stylus and Pure White paint, place a dot at top of eye.

❺ Using stylus and Dark Gray-Blue paint, dot ends of lines on body and wings.
❻ Repeat all of above steps for other side of duck.

Finishing

Use adhesive/sealant to assemble.
❶ Use a damp cotton swab to remove remaining transfer lines.
❷ Using glaze brush, apply three coats of water-based varnish to all sides of pieces. Let each coat dry separately.
❸ Apply glue to one end of each dowel and insert into holes in body piece.
❹ Apply glue to other end of dowels and insert into holes in feet. Duck walks with his/her toes pointed outward.
❺ Glue wings to body. Refer to pattern for placement.
❻ Attach eye hooks to top of head and tail. Using pliers, attach a chain length to each hook. Adjust lengths as needed.
❼ Thread bell onto ribbon. Tie ribbon around neck with a bow.

Additional Idea

💜 Dress Quacky Doodle in a bright yellow raincoat, rain hat, and bright red miniature galoshes to celebrate April showers.

buttercup
COW

Designed by Linda Alexander

Buttercup was the first animal we designed for our Welcome Sign. She remains a favorite.
Read General Instructions before beginning any project. Trace Buttercup Cow patterns on pg. 27 onto tracing paper, omitting slash marks which indicate shaded areas.

Specific Materials Needed

7" x 10" of ¾"-thick clear pine (body)
6" x 12" of ½"-thick clear pine (legs)
Two 1½" lengths of ¼"-wide brass chain
Two brass eye hooks, ¼" dia.
Scroll saw
Drill and ⅛"-dia. bit
All-purpose water-base sealer
Water-base varnish
Colored transfer paper
Stylus
Disposable sponge brush (1" wide)
Script liner brush (#10/0)
Round brush (#1)
Flat brush (#8)
Glaze brush (¾" wide)
Needle-nose pliers
Cotton swab

4" sq. of black ultrasuede (ears)
24" length of ⅛"-dia. black cording (tail)
12" of ¼"-wide pink satin ribbon
1"-dia. brass cowbell
Adhesive/sealant

Acrylic Paint Palette

Pale Pink
Pink
Light Gray-Blue
Medium Yellow-Brown
Light Tan
Dove Gray
Black
Soft White

Preparation

❶ Using patterns and scroll saw, cut body and legs. Round edges. Using pattern, cut out ears.
❷ Using drill and bit, drill a hole ¼" deep in each side of head for ears and a hole on back edge for tail. See pattern for placement.
❸ Prepare wood for painting, referring to Wood Preparation on pg. 8.
❹ Using a disposable sponge brush, wash all sides of body and legs with a mixture of ⅓ Soft White paint, ⅓ water, and ⅓ all-purpose water-base sealer. Usually two coats are needed. Let each coat dry separately. Lightly paper-sand after each coat.
❺ Match traced outline of body design with wood piece. Using stylus and transfer paper, trace design. Repeat for a set of legs.
❻ Turn tracing paper over so that designs are reversed. Retrace designs onto other side of body and other set of legs.

When painting dimensional items, paint one side and edges; let dry. Paint remaining side. When painting black spots on cow, join spots on each side by carrying color across edges. Refer to patterns and photo for placement of shading and details.

Base Coating

Use flat brush for steps 1–2.
❶ Using Black paint, paint hooves, spots on body, and legs with three coats. Let each coat dry separately.
❷ Using Pale Pink paint, paint udder with three coats.

❸ Using round brush and Light Tan paint, paint eye.

Shading

Use flat brush side loaded with paint. Refer to slash marks on pattern for placement.

❶ Using Medium Yellow-Brown paint, shade lower edge of eye.

❷ Using Dove Gray paint, shade area in front of eye, following curve of eyeball, and shade U-shaped nostril area.

❸ Using Pink paint, shade top of udder next to body.

Lining

Use script liner brush.

❶ Using Soft White paint, place a thin line between gray shading and eye, following curve of eye.

❷ Using Light Gray-Blue paint, outline top edge of shaded area of nostril and line mouth. Carry mouth line across front edge to other side of cow.

❸ Using Black paint, place two eyelashes at top of eye and one at bottom of eye. Extend lines to outline back and bottom of eye.

Details

Read Tips and Tricks on pg. 9 before beginning. Use stylus.

❶ Using Black paint, place pupil in upper part of eye, and a dot at end of each eyelash and at back corner of eye. Let dry.

❷ Using Light Gray-Blue paint, place a small dot at end of mouth line.

❸ Using Soft White paint, place a small dot at top of pupil.

❹ Repeat above steps for remaining side of cow.

Finishing

Use adhesive/sealant to assemble.

❶ Use a damp cotton swab to remove remaining transfer lines.

❷ Using glaze brush, apply three coats of water-base varnish to all sides of pieces. Let each coat dry separately.

❸ Cut off end of cotton swab. Roll an ear piece around shaft. Insert a drop of adhesive/sealant into ear hole. Insert rolled ear piece. Repeat for other ear. Let dry.

❹ Cut cording into 8" lengths. Align ends and tie together with an overhand knot. Trim end of cord close to knot.

❺ Braid cord for 4". Tie ends together with an overhand knot. Trim ends, leaving a ½" tail.

❻ Insert a drop of glue into tail hole. Push trimmed end of tail into hole. Let dry.

❼ Glue legs to body. Refer to photo for placement.

❽ Attach eye hooks to top of head and rump. Using pliers, attach a chain length to each hook. Adjust lengths as needed to hang.

❾ Thread bell onto ribbon. Tie ribbon around neck with a bow.

ribbitt. frog

Designed by Lorna McRoden

When people call and ask what I'm doing, I always hear a surprised laugh when I answer, "I'm painting frogs!"

Read General Instructions before beginning any project. Trace Ribbit T. Frog patterns on pg. 26 onto tracing paper, omitting slash marks which indicate shaded areas.

Specific Materials Needed

4" x 9" of ¾"-thick clear pine (body)
6" x 12" of ½"-thick clear pine (legs)
Two 2" lengths of ¼"-wide brass chain
Two brass eye hooks, ¼" dia.
Scroll saw
All-purpose water-base sealer
Disposable sponge brush (1" wide)
Colored transfer paper
Stylus
Round brush (#1)
¼"-, ⅜"-, and ⅝"-dia. wood dowels (4")
Flat brush (#8)
Script liner brush (#10/0)
Glaze brush (¾" wide)
Water-base varnish
Needle-nose pliers
12" of ¼"-wide blue satin ribbon
Adhesive/sealant

Acrylic Paint Palette

Dark Pink
Creamy Yellow
Orange
Olive Green
Medium Dark Teal
Black
Pure White

Preparation

❶ Using patterns and scroll saw, cut wood pieces. Round edges.

❷ Prepare wood for painting, referring to Wood Preparation on pg. 8.

❸ Using a disposable sponge brush, wash all sides of wood items with a mixture of ⅓ Olive Green paint, ⅓ water, and ⅓ all-purpose water-base sealer. Usually two coats are needed. Let each coat dry separately. Lightly paper-sand after each coat.

❹ Match traced outline of body design with wood piece. Using stylus and transfer paper, trace design. Turn tracing paper over so

that design is reversed. Retrace design onto other side of body.
❺ Match traced outline of legs design with wood pieces. Using stylus and transfer paper, trace designs. Turn tracing paper over so that design is reversed. Retrace design onto other set of legs.

When painting dimensional items, paint one side and edges; let dry. Paint remaining side. Refer to Colored Example on right side of page, patterns, and photo for placement of shading and details.

Lining

Using fine script liner brush and Medium Dark Teal paint, paint thin lines between toes and line dividing back leg and mouth. Carry mouth line across front edge to other side.

Shading

Using flat brush side loaded with Dark Pink paint, float curving cheek line.

Details

Read Tips and Tricks on pg. 9 before beginning.
❶ Using end of ⅝"-dia. dowel dipped in Creamy Yellow paint, make a dot for eye. Let dry.
❷ Using script liner brush and Orange paint, line a half circle along bottom edge of eye.
❸ Using end of ⅜"-dia. dowel dipped in Black paint, place a dot in middle of creamy yellow dot.

❹ Using end of ¼"-dia. dowel dipped in Pure White paint, place dots on legs and body.
❺ Using fine script liner brush and Black paint, outline outside edge of eye.
❻ Using stylus and Medium Dark Teal paint, place dots at ends of lines between toes and at top of dividing line in back leg.
❼ Using stylus and Pure White paint, place two descending-sized dots at top of pupil.
❽ Repeat all of above steps for other side of frog.

Finishing

Use adhesive/sealant to assemble.
❶ Use a damp cotton swab to remove remaining transfer lines.
❷ Using glaze brush, apply three coats of water-base varnish to all sides of pieces. Let each coat dry separately.
❸ Glue legs to body. Refer to photo for placement.
❹ Attach eye hooks to top of head and rump. Using pliers, attach a chain length to each hook. Adjust lengths as needed.
❺ Tie ribbon tightly around neck with a bow.

Additional Idea

♥ Place a small crown on Ribbit T. Frog's head and write "Kiss Me" on the sign.

Details ❶

Details ❷

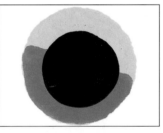
Details ❸

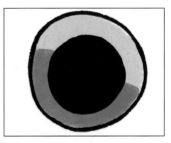
Details ❺

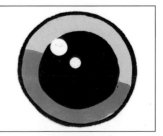
Details ❼
Ribbit T. Frog Colored Example (eyes)

25

Enlarge patterns 125%.

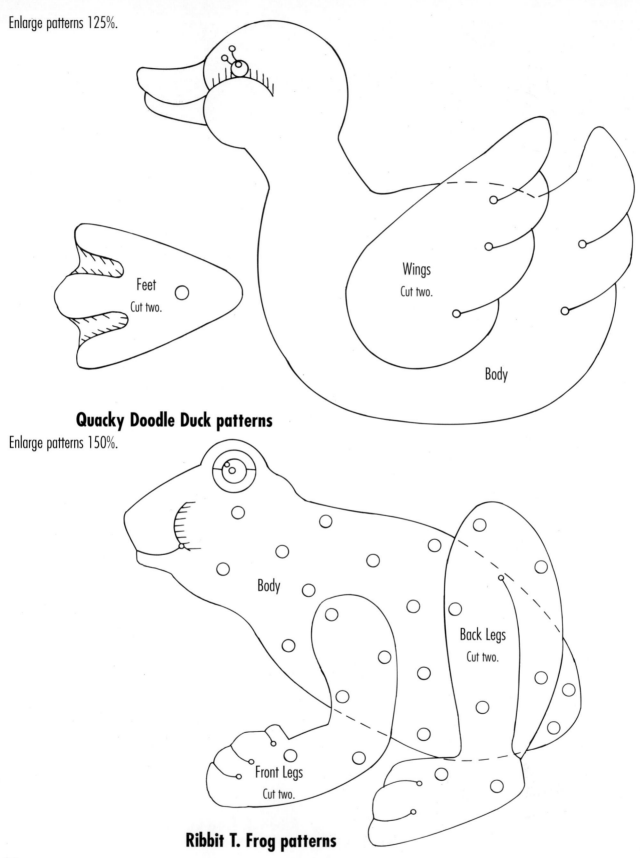

Quacky Doodle Duck patterns

Enlarge patterns 150%.

Ribbit T. Frog patterns

Enlarge patterns 120%.

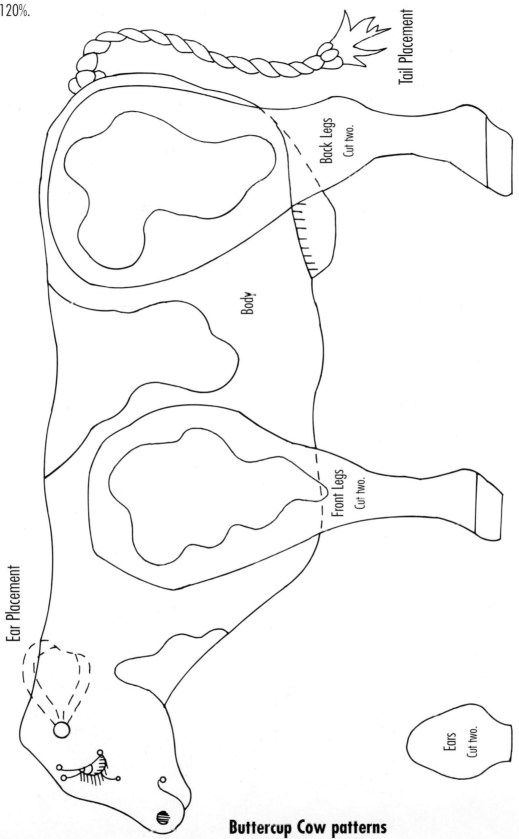

Tail Placement

Back Legs
Cut two.

Body

Front Legs
Cut two.

Ear Placement

Ears
Cut two.

Buttercup Cow patterns

holiday
Welcome

Designed by Linda Alexander

Read General Instructions before beginning any project. Trace Holiday Welcome pattern on pg. 31 and Backboard pattern on pg. 20 onto tracing paper.

Specific Materials Needed

4" x 12" of ¾"-thick clear pine (backboard)
3" x 11" of ½"-thick clear plywood (sign)
Band saw
Two 1½"-long drywall screws
Two ½"-dia. brass cup hooks
All-purpose water-base sealer
Disposable sponge brush (1" wide)
Colored transfer paper
Stylus
⅛"- and ¼"-dia. wood dowels (4")
Script liner brush (#1)
Glaze brush (¾" wide)
Water-base varnish

Acrylic Paint Palette

Bright Red
Dark Wine Red
Christmas Green
Teal Green
Soft White

Preparation

❶ Using pattern, cut out backboard with band saw. Round edges. Using pattern, cut out sign with band saw.
❷ Prepare wood for painting, referring to Wood Preparation on pg. 8.
❸ Using a disposable sponge brush, wash all sides of wood items with a mixture of ⅓ Soft White paint, ⅓ water, and ⅓ all-purpose water-base sealer. Usually two coats are needed. Let each coat dry separately. Lightly paper-sand after each coat.
❹ Match traced outline of Holiday Welcome pattern with wood piece. Using stylus and transfer paper, trace design. Turn wood piece over. Retrace design.
❺ Match traced outline of backboard design with wood piece. Using stylus and transfer paper, trace design.

When painting dimensional items, paint one side and edges; let dry. Paint remaining side. Refer to patterns and photo for placement of details.

Lining

Using script liner brush and Christmas Green paint, line lettering and decorative and scalloped lines on sign and backboard.

Lettering and Details

Read Tips and Tricks on pg. 9 before beginning steps 2–5.
❶ Using end of ⅛"-dia. dowel and Teal Green paint, dot ends of all letters.
❷ Using end of ¼"-dia. dowel and Bright Red paint, make hearts to join scalloped lines at center top and bottom edges of backboard, and at center top edge of sign.
❸ Using end of ⅛"-dia. dowel and handle ends of smaller-sized brushes and Bright Red paint, make three descending-sized dots at ends of straight lines on backboard and five descending-sized dots at ends of curved lines on sign.
❹ Using end of ⅛"-dia. dowel and Bright Red paint, dot first, center, and end points of scalloped line below lettering.
❺ Using end of ⅛"-dia. dowel and Dark Wine Red paint, dot remaining points of scalloped lines on both backboard and sign.
❻ Repeat all of above steps for other side of sign.

Finishing

❶ Use a damp cotton swab to remove remaining transfer lines.
❷ Using glaze brush, apply three coats of water-based varnish to all sides of pieces. Let each coat dry separately.
❸ Using drywall screws, join backboard and sign as indicated on pattern.
❹ Attach cup hooks to bottom edge of sign 3¼" from each end.

Additional Ideas

❤ Glue Christmas trees or Santa, sleigh, and reindeer to top edge of Holiday sign.

❤ For a change of pace, wrap backboard with twinkling Christmas lights or a festive garland.

❤ Make a welcome sign for every holiday with appropriate saying and colors.

m e r r y
krisMoose

Designed by Lorna McRoden

Krismoose is glad to welcome the holidays to your home.

Read General Instructions before beginning any project. Trace Merry Krismoose patterns on pg. 32 onto tracing paper, omitting slash marks which indicate shaded areas.

8" x 12" of ½"-thick clear pine (legs)
4" x 7" of ¼"-thick clear plywood (antlers)
4" x 10" of ¾"-thick clear pine (body)
3" sq. of tan ultrasuede (ears)
Scroll saw
Drill and ⅛"- and ¼"-dia. bits
Two ¼"-dia. brass eye hooks
Two 2" lengths of ¼"-wide brass chain
Stain controller/wood sealer
Oak-colored stain
All-purpose water-base sealer
Stylus
Colored transfer paper
3 unfinished wood buttons (½" dia.)
Red sewing thread
Disposable sponge brushes (1" wide)
Script liner brush (#10/0)
Round brush (#1)
Flat brush (#8)
Glaze brush (¾" wide)
Water-base varnish
Adhesive/sealant
Cotton swab
Needle-nose pliers
½ yd. of ⅛"-wide red satin ribbon
Two ½"-dia. brass cowbells

Bright Red
Dark Wine Red
Light Butter Yellow
Soft Light Blue
Medium Light Blue
Medium Brown
Chocolate Brown
Black
Soft White

❶ Using patterns and scroll saw, cut wood pieces. Round edges of body and leg pieces. Using pattern, cut out ears.

❷ Using drill and ¼"-dia. bit, drill a ¼"-deep hole in each side of head for ears. Refer to pattern for placement.

❸ Using drill and ⅛"-dia. bit, drill a hole through antlers on each side. Refer to pattern for placement.

❹ Prepare wood for staining and painting, referring to Wood Preparation on pg. 8.

❺ Using a disposable sponge brush, seal and stain all sides of moose's body and legs. Paper-sand when dry.

❻ Using a disposable sponge brush, wash all sides of antlers with a mixture of ⅓ Light Butter Yellow paint, ⅓ water, and ⅓ all-purpose water-base sealer with two coats. Let each coat dry separately. Lightly paper-sand after each coat.

❼ Match traced outline of each body design with wood piece. Using stylus and transfer paper, trace design, omitting stitch lines and flap lines, which will be traced later. Turn tracing paper over so that designs are reversed. Retrace designs onto other side of body and other legs.

❽ Using a disposable sponge brush, paint long johns onto all sides of moose's body (over stain) with a mixture of ⅔ Bright Red paint and ⅓ water. Carry color across edges onto other side of each wood piece. Two coats will be needed. Let each coat dry separately. Lightly paper-sand after each coat.

❾ Match traced outline of each body design with wood piece. Using stylus and transfer paper, trace stitch lines and flap lines. Turn tracing paper over so that designs are reversed. Trace lines onto other side of body and other legs.

When painting mouth and stitch lines on moose, join lines on each side by carrying color across edges. Refer to patterns and photo for placement of shading and details.

Refer to slash marks on pattern for placement of shading. Use two coats for base painting.

❶ Using flat brush and Black paint, base-paint hooves.

❷ Using round brush and Soft Light Blue paint, base-paint all of eye. Let dry.

❸ Using round brush and Black paint, paint pupil.

❹ Using flat brush side loaded with Medium Light Blue paint, shade lower edge of eyeball.

❺ Using flat brush side loaded with Medium Brown paint, shade half circle in front of eye and nostril area.

❻ Using round brush and Chocolate Brown paint, base-paint gap area in flap.

❼ Using flat brush side loaded with Dark Wine Red paint, shade along edge of flap line.

❽ Using round brush and Soft White paint, base-paint all sides of buttons.

Lining and Dots

Refer to pattern for placement and to Tips and Tricks on pg. 9.
❶ Using script liner brush and Soft White paint, outline front edge of eyeball.
❷ Using script liner brush and Black paint, line mouth, outline back edge of eyeball, and line eyelashes.
❸ Using stylus and Black paint, place a dot at end of each eyelash, at back corner of eye, and at end of mouth line.
❹ Using stylus and Soft White paint, place a tiny dot in pupil.
❺ Using script liner brush and Soft White paint, line stitch lines on long johns.

Repeat all steps in Base Coating and Shading, and Lining and Dots for other side of moose.

Details

Using red thread, stitch center of buttons.

Finishing

Use adhesive/sealant to assemble.
❶ Use a damp cotton swab to remove remaining transfer lines.
❷ Using glaze brush, apply three coats of water-base varnish to all sides of pieces. Let each coat dry separately.

❸ Cut off end of cotton swab. Roll an ear piece around shaft. Insert a drop of adhesive/sealant into ear hole. Insert rolled ear. Repeat for other ear. Let dry.
❹ Cut ribbon in half. Thread a bell onto one length of ribbon. Thread ribbon through one of antler holes. Tie ribbon into a bow. Repeat for remaining ribbon and bell.
❺ Glue legs to body. Insert and glue antlers into slot in head. Let dry completely.
❻ Attach eye hooks to top edges of shoulder and rump. Using pliers, attach a chain length to each hook. Adjust lengths as needed.
❼ Glue buttons to long johns. Refer to pattern for placement.

Additional Ideas

♥ Glue skis, a snowboard, a sleigh, or a toboggan to Krismoose's feet.

♥ For just a touch of whimsy, paint Krismoose's nose red (just like Rudolph!).

♥ Decorate Krismoose's antlers with miniature ornaments instead of bells.

♥ Make Krismoose's antlers to look like Christmas trees.

♥ Give Krismoose a nightcap to match his long johns.

Enlarge pattern 115%.

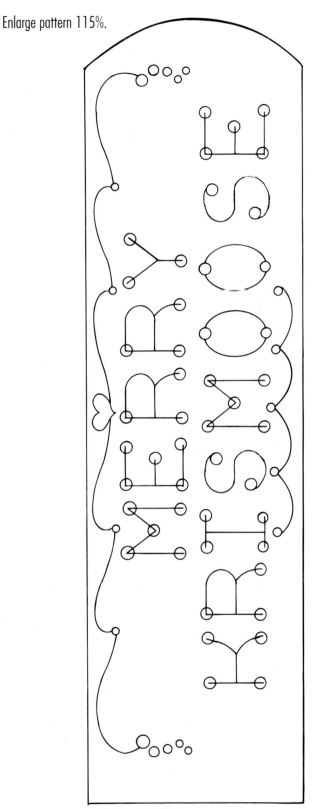

Holiday Welcome pattern
(Backboard pattern on pg. 20)

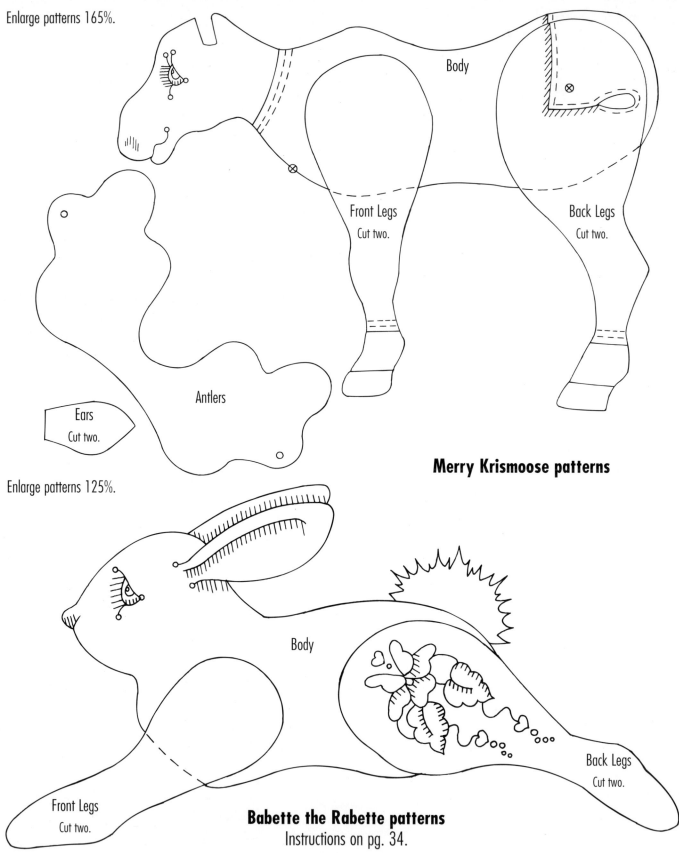

Enlarge patterns 165%.

Body

Front Legs
Cut two.

Back Legs
Cut two.

Antlers

Ears
Cut two.

Merry Krismoose patterns

Enlarge patterns 125%.

Body

Front Legs
Cut two.

Back Legs
Cut two.

Babette the Rabette patterns
Instructions on pg. 34.

32

babette the
rabette

Designed by Lorna McRoden

Babette will graciously welcome all of your guests.

Read General Instructions before beginning any project. Trace Babette the Rabette patterns on pg. 32 onto tracing paper, omitting slash marks which indicate shaded areas.

5" x 7" of ¾"-thick clear pine (body)
5" x 9" of ½"-thick clear pine (legs)
2 -dia. pom pom (tail)
Scroll saw
Two ¼"-dia. brass eye hooks
Two 3" lengths of ¼"-wide brass chain
All-purpose water-base sealer
Stylus
Colored transfer paper
2 yds. of ¼"-wide light mauve satin ribbon
2 small artificial violets (approx. 1¼" dia.)
2 small variegated artificial ivy leaves (¾" wide)
⅛"-dia. wood dowel (4")
Disposable sponge brush (1" wide)
Script liner brush (#10/0)

Round brush (#1)
Flat brush (#8)
Glaze brush (¾" wide)
Water-base varnish
Adhesive/sealant
Needle-nose pliers

Acrylic Paint Palette

Light Rose Pink
Dark Pink
Butter Yellow
Pale Green
Dark Yellow-Green
Medium Dark Teal
Light Violet
Violet-Blue
Light Blue-Gray
Light Tan
Medium Yellow-Brown
Dove Gray
Black
Soft White
Pure White

Preparation

❶ Using patterns and scroll saw, cut wood pieces. Round edges.
❷ Prepare wood for painting, referring to Wood Preparation on pg. 8.

❸ Using disposable sponge brush, wash all sides of wood items with a mixture of ⅓ Soft White paint, ⅓ water, and ⅓ all-purpose water-base sealer. Usually two coats are needed. Let each coat dry separately. Lightly paper-sand after each coat.
❹ Match traced outline of body design with wood piece. Using stylus and transfer paper, trace head. Turn tracing paper over so that design is reversed. Retrace design onto other side of body.
❺ Match traced outline of back leg design with wood piece. Using stylus and transfer paper, trace flower motif.

When painting dimensional items, paint one side and edges; let dry. Paint remaining side. When painting nose, join areas on each side by carrying color across front edge. Refer to patterns and photo for placement of shading and details.

Rabbit's Head

Refer to slash marks on pattern for placement of shading. Use two coats for base painting.

❶ Using round brush and Light Tan paint, base-paint all of eye. Let dry.
❷ Using round brush and Black paint, paint pupil.
❸ Using flat brush side loaded with Medium Yellow-Brown paint, shade lower edge of eyeball.
❹ Using flat brush side loaded with Dove Gray paint, shade half circle in front of eye, along top of head, and between and below ears.
❺ Using flat brush side loaded with Light Rose Pink paint, shade inside of ear and tip of nose.

Lining and Dots

Use script liner brush for steps 1–5. Refer to pattern for placement and to Tips and Tricks on pg. 9 before beginning.
❶ Using Soft White paint, outline front edge of eyeball.
❷ Using Light Blue-Gray paint, outline back of eyeball and line eyelashes, along top of head, and above and below front ear.
❸ Using Light Blue-Gray paint, place a dot at end of each eyelash, at back corner of eye, and at end of lines on front ear.
❹ Using Soft White paint, place a tiny dot in pupil.
❺ Using Dark Pink paint, line top edge of pink area in ear and along bottom edge of pink area on nose.

Repeat all of the steps in Rabbit's Head, and Lining and Dots for the other side of rabbit.

Refer to slash marks on pattern for placement of shading and to Tips and Tricks on pg. 9 for details.

❶ Using script liner brush and Medium Dark Teal paint, line tendrils.

❷ Using round brush and Pale Green paint, base-paint leaves, using two coats.

❸ Using round brush and Light Violet paint, base-paint flower petals, using two coats.

❹ Using flat brush side loaded with Dark Yellow-Green paint, shade leaves along right edges and along left side of midveins.

❺ Using flat brush side loaded with Violet-Blue paint, shade top edge of three bottom petals.

❻ Using flat brush side loaded with Pure White paint, highlight leaves along left edges, and along right side of midveins; highlight three lower flowers' petals along scalloped bottom edges and two upper petals along scalloped edges.

❼ Using stylus and Butter Yellow paint, place a dot in center of flower. Let dry.

❽ Using stylus and Black paint, place a smaller dot near top of yellow dot. Let dry.

❾ Using stylus and Pure White paint, place a small dot at each side of yellow dot. Pull these dots up into a teardrop shape, joining them at top of black dot.

❿ Using stylus and Light Rose Pink paint, make a heart at end of each tendril and a heart between two upper petals.

Using stylus and Pale Green paint, place four descending-sized dots below each of lower hearts and one dot below upper heart.

Finishing

Use adhesive/sealant to assemble.

❶ Use a damp cotton swab to remove remaining transfer lines.

❷ Using glaze brush, apply three coats of water-base varnish to all sides of pieces. Let each coat dry separately.

❸ Glue legs to body.

❹ Glue pom pom to rump.

❺ Attach eye hooks to top of head and just in front of tail. Using pliers, attach a chain length to each hook. Adjust lengths as needed.

❻ Using ribbon, tie a multiloop bow around neck. Glue base of artificial ivy and violets to knot of bow.

Additional Ideas

❤ Write "Hoppy Easter" on Babette the Rabette's welcome sign.

❤ Write "Have a Purr-fect Halloween" on Miss Kitty's welcome sign.

❤ Write "Hogs & Kisses" on Rosebud Pig's Valentine's Day welcome sign.

miss kitty

Designed by Lorna McRoden

Read General Instructions before beginning any project. Trace Miss Kitty patterns on pg. 38 onto tracing paper, omitting slash marks which indicate shaded areas.

Specific Materials Needed

8" sq. of ¾"-thick clear pine (body)
4" x 15" of ½"-thick clear pine (legs)
Scroll saw
Drill and ⅛"-dia. bit
Two ¼"-dia. brass eye hooks
Two 3" lengths of ¼"-wide brass chain
All-purpose water-base sealer
Stylus
White transfer paper
Disposable sponge brush (1" wide)
Script liner brush (#10/0)
Round brush (#1)
Flat brush (#8)
Glaze brush (¾" wide)
Water-base varnish
Adhesive/sealant
Needle-nose pliers
Wooden mouse (1½" long)
1"-dia. painted resin Jack o' Lantern face
2 yds. of ¼"-wide orange satin ribbon
1" length of artificial greenery

Acrylic Paint Palette

Light Rose Pink
Dark Peach
Orange
Pale Green
Light Yellow-Green
Medium Yellow-Green
Dark Yellow-Green
Charcoal
Black
Soft White

Preparation

❶ Using pattern and scroll saw, cut wood pieces. Round edges.

❷ Using drill and bit, drill a ¼"-deep hole in mouth area (on front edge of body).

❸ Prepare wood for painting, referring to Wood Preparation on pg. 8.

❹ Using disposable sponge brush, wash all sides of wood items with a mixture of ⅓ Charcoal paint, ⅓ water, and ⅓ all-purpose water-base sealer. Usually two coats are needed.

Let each coat dry separately. Lightly paper-sand after each coat.

❺ Match traced outline of body design with wood piece. Using stylus and transfer paper, trace face. Turn tracing paper over so that design is reversed. Retrace design onto other side of body.

❻ Match traced outline of back leg design with wood piece. Using stylus and transfer paper, trace design, omitting Jack o' Lantern face (to be traced later).

When painting dimensional items, paint one side and edges; let dry. Paint remaining side. When painting nose, join areas on each side by carrying color across front edge. Refer to Colored Example on right side of page, patterns, and photo for place-ment of shading and details.

Kitty's Head

Refer to slash marks on patterns for placement of shading. Use two coats for base painting.

❶ Using round brush and Light Yellow-Green paint, base-paint all of eye. Let dry.

❷ Using flat brush side loaded with Medium Yellow-Green paint, shade lower edge of eyeball.

❸ Using round brush and Black paint, paint pupil of eye.

❹ Using round brush and Light Rose Pink paint, base-paint inside of ear and nose area.

❺ Using flat brush side loaded with Black paint, shade half circle in front of eye, under and between ears, and between hip and tail.

❻ Using script liner brush and Soft White paint, outline front edge of eyeball, paint eyelashes, line mouth, place a line between hip and tail, a line at top of head, one line between ears, and outline pink area in ear.

❼ Using stylus and Soft White paint, place a tiny dot in pupil, a dot at end of each eyelash, at back corner of eye, and at end of mouth line.

Repeat steps in Kitty's Head for other side of kitty.

Pumpkin

Refer to patterns for placement. Use two coats of paint for base painting.

❶ Using round brush and Orange paint, base-paint pumpkin, leaving a fine line between areas.

❷ Using round brush and Pale Green paint, base-paint leaves and stem of pumpkin.

❸ Using fine script liner brush and Pale Green paint, line tendrils behind pumpkin.

❹ Using handle end of round brush and Soft White paint, place three descending-sized dots at end of each tendril.

Shading and Highlighting

Refer to photograph and slash marks on patterns for placement of shading.

❶ Using flat brush side loaded with Dark Yellow-Green paint, shade leaves along bottom edges and above midveins.

❷ Using flat brush side loaded with Dark Peach paint, shade along fine lines between areas on pumpkin.

❸ Using flat brush side loaded with Soft White paint, highlight along top edge of each leaf, out-side edges of pumpkin, and along Dark Peach vertical lines of pumpkin.

❹ Using script liner brush and Soft White paint, line midvein of each leaf and outline top of pumpkin stem.

Jack o' Lantern Face

❶ Match traced outline of back leg design with its wood piece. Using stylus and transfer paper, trace face of Jack o' Lantern onto pumpkin.

❷ Using round brush and Black paint, base-paint face using two coats.

❸ Using stylus and Soft White paint, make a tiny dot in each eye.

Finishing

Use adhesive/sealant to assemble.

❶ Use a damp cotton swab to remove remaining transfer lines.

❷ Using glaze brush, apply three coats of water-base varnish to all sides of pieces. Let each coat dry separately.

❸ Glue legs to body.

❹ Attach eye hooks to top of head and tail. Using pliers, attach a length of chain to each hook. Adjust lengths as needed.

❺ Using ribbon, tie a multiloop bow around neck.

❻ Glue greenery to knot in bow. Glue resin Jack o' Lantern over greenery. Glue end of mouse's tail to mouth.

Kitty's Head ❶

Kitty's Head ❷

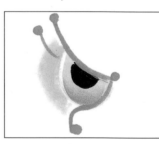

Kitty's Head ❸, ❺, and ❻

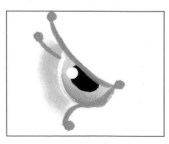

Kitty's Head ❼

Miss Kitty Colored Example (eyes)

r o s e b u d
p i g

Designed by Lorna McRoden & John Alexander

Rosebud is as sweet as a rose. Read General Instructions before beginning any project. Trace Rosebud Pig patterns on pg. 38 onto tracing paper, omitting slash marks which indicate shaded areas.

Specific Materials Needed

5" x 10" of ¾"-thick clear pine (body)
5" x 10" of ½"-thick clear pine (legs)
2" of ⅛"-dia. pink rattail cord (tail)
3"-sq. pink ultrasuede (ears)
Scroll saw
Drill and ¼"-dia. bit
Two ¼"-dia. brass eye hooks
Two 2" lengths of ¼"-wide brass chain
All-purpose water-base sealer
Stylus
Colored transfer paper
⅛"-dia. wood dowel (4")
Disposable sponge brush (1" wide)
Script liner brush (#10/0)
Round brush (#1)
Flat brush (#8)
Glaze brush (¾" wide)
Water-base varnish
Adhesive/sealant

Needle-nose pliers
2 yds. of ¼"-wide pink satin ribbon
2 small artificial rosebuds
Small spray of artificial baby's breath
Cotton swab

Acrylic Paint Palette

Pale Pink
Pink
Dark Pink
Soft Light Blue
Medium Light Blue
Black
Soft White

Preparation

❶ Using patterns and scroll saw, cut wood pieces. Round edges. Using pattern, cut out ears.
❷ Using drill and bit, drill a ¼"-deep hole in each side of head for ears and a hole on back edge for tail. Refer to pattern for placement.
❸ Prepare wood for painting, referring to Wood Preparation on pg. 8.
❹ Using a disposable sponge brush, wash all sides of wood

items with a mixture of ⅓ Pale Pink paint, ⅓ water, and ⅓ all-purpose water-base sealer. Usually two coats are needed. Let each coat dry separately. Lightly paper-sand after each coat.
❺ Match traced outline of body design with wood piece. Using stylus and transfer paper, trace face and heart pattern. Turn tracing paper over so that design is reversed. Retrace design onto other side of body.
❻ Match traced outline of each leg design with wood piece. Using stylus and transfer paper, trace designs.

When painting dimensional items, paint one side and edges; let dry. Paint remaining side. When painting mouth lines and lines on feet, join on each side by carrying color across front edge. Refer to Colored Example on pg. 38, patterns, and photo for placement of shading and details.

Base Coating and Shading

Refer to slash marks on patterns for placement of shading. Use two coats for base painting.

❶ Using round brush and Soft Light Blue paint, base-paint all of eye. Let dry.
❷ Using round brush and Black paint, paint pupil of eye.
❸ Using flat brush side loaded with Medium Light Blue paint, shade lower edge of eyeball.
❹ Using flat brush side loaded with Pink paint, shade half circle on cheek.

Lining and Dots

Use script liner brush for steps 1 and 4 and stylus for steps 2, 3, and 5. Refer to patterns for placement and to Tips and Tricks on pg. 9 before beginning.

❶ Using Black paint, outline eyeball and paint eyelashes.
❷ Using Black paint, place a dot at end of each eyelash.
❸ Using Soft White paint, place a tiny dot in pupil.
❹ Using Dark Pink paint, line mouth and lines on feet.
❺ Using Dark Pink paint, dot ends of mouth line and lines on feet.
❻ Using end of dowel and Pink paint, paint hearts.

Repeat all steps in Base Coating and Shading, and Lining and Dots for other side of pig.

Finishing

Use adhesive/sealant to assemble.

❶ Use a damp cotton swab to remove remaining transfer lines.
❷ Using glaze brush, apply three coats of water-base varnish

to all sides of pieces. Let each coat dry separately.

❸ Cut off end of cotton swab. Roll an ear piece around shaft. Insert a drop of glue into ear hole. Insert rolled ear. Repeat for other ear.

❹ Fold rattail cord in half. Tie together using an overhand knot. Apply glue to cut ends. Push ends into hole in rump.

❺ Glue legs to body.

❻ Attach eye hooks to neck and rump. Using pliers, attach a chain length to each hook. Adjust lengths as needed.

❼ Using ribbon, tie a multiloop bow around neck. Glue artificial rosebud and baby's breath to knot of bow.

Base Coating and Shading ❷

Base Coating and Shading ❸

Lining and Dots ❶ and ❷

Lining and Dots ❸
Rosebud Pig Colored Example (eyes)

Enlarge patterns 155%.

Body

Back Legs
Cut two.

Front Legs
Cut two.

Miss Kitty patterns

Enlarge patterns 145%.

Body

Front Legs
Cut two.

Back Legs
Cut two.

Ears
Cut two.

Rosebud Pig patterns

s t i t c h e s the
b u n n y

Designed by Lorna McRoden

These pull toys are meant for display only and should not be used by children under four.

Read General Instructions before beginning any project. Trace Stitches the Bunny patterns on pgs. 41 and 42 onto tracing paper, omitting slash marks which indicate shaded areas.

7" x 10" of ¾"-thick clear pine (body)

Two 3¾" lengths of ¼"-dia. wood dowel (axle)

Four ⅝"-high wood spools with ¼"-dia. hole in center (spacers)

Four ⅝"-high wood mini candle cups with ¼"-dia. hole (hubs)

Four 2"-dia. wheels (¼"-dia. hole)

Scroll saw

Drill and ¼"-dia. bit

Stain controller/wood sealer

Oak-colored wood stain

All-purpose water-base sealer

Stylus

Colored transfer paper

Disposable sponge brushes (1" wide)

Flat brush (#8 and #12)

Round brush (#1)

Script liner brush (#10/0)

Clear matte spray acrylic finish

1 yd. of ⅛"-wide green satin ribbon

1"-dia. brass bell

Adhesive/sealant

Acrylic Paint Palette

Dark Pink

Light Rose Pink

Soft Light Blue

Medium Blue

Medium Light Blue

Medium Dark Blue

Medium Gray-Blue

Light Violet-Blue

Lilac

Medium Dark Teal

Medium Yellow-Brown

Light Tan

Dove Gray

Black

Soft White

Preparation

❶ Using pattern and scroll saw, cut wood pieces. Round edges.

❷ Using drill and bit, drill a hole through base of each leg ¼" from bottom edge.

❸ Prepare wood for staining and painting, referring to Wood Preparation on pg. 8.

❹ Using a disposable brush and oak stain, seal and stain all sides of wheels and spool spacers. Paper-sand when dry.

❺ Using a disposable brush, wash all sides of bunny with a mixture of ⅓ Soft White paint, ⅓ water, and ⅓ all-purpose water-base sealer. Usually two coats are needed. Let dry. Paper-sand after each coat.

❻ Using #12 flat brush and Medium Dark Teal paint, paint wheel hubs.

❼ Match traced outline of Left Side Body Pattern with wood piece. Using stylus and transfer paper, trace design. Turn over.

❽ Match traced outline of Right Side Body Pattern with wood piece. Using stylus and transfer paper, trace design.

To paint dimensional items, paint one side and edges; let dry. Paint remaining side. When shading nose, join shaded areas on each side by carrying color across front edge. Refer to patterns and photo for placement of shading and details.

Base Coating and Shading

Refer to slash marks on patterns for placement of shading.

❶ Using round brush and Light Tan paint, base-paint eye using two coats. Let dry.

❷ Using round brush and Black paint, paint pupil of eye using two coats.

❸ Using #8 flat brush side loaded with Medium Yellow-Brown paint, shade lower edge of eyeball.

❹ Using flat brush side loaded with Dove Gray paint, shade half circle in front of eye, under and between ears, under chin, and between hip and tail.

❺ Using flat brush side loaded with Light Rose Pink paint, shade inside of ear and nose.

Details

Use script liner brush for steps 2–4 and stylus for steps 1 and 5. Refer to patterns for placement.

❶ Using Soft White paint, place a tiny dot in pupil.

❷ Using Medium Gray-Blue paint, paint eyelashes, and line between ears, below front ear, along top of head, under chin, and between hip and tail.

❸ Using Dark Pink paint, paint a line along top of pink-shaded area in ear.

❹ Using Medium Blue paint, paint stitch lines around outside edges of body and top of ears.

❺ Using Medium Gray-Blue paint, place a dot at end of each eyelash, one at back corner of eye, and one at ends of lines above and below front ear.

Repeat all of the steps in Base Coating and Shading, and Details for the other side of bunny.

Patches—Left Side of Bunny

Use round brush for steps 1–3, script liner brush for steps 4 and 6, and stylus for steps 7, 10, and 11. Refer to pattern for placement. Use two coats to base-paint.

❶ Using Light Violet-Blue paint, base-paint small heart patch.

❷ Using Soft Light Blue paint, basc-paint diamond-shaped area of large patch.

❸ Using Lilac paint, base-paint remaining areas of large patch.

❹ Using Black paint, make small hearts in top right-hand section of large patch.

❺ Using Medium Light Blue paint, line straight stitches in diamond-shaped area of large patch.

❻ Using Medium Dark Blue paint, line stitches on large patch and line hanging threads.

❼ Using Soft Light Blue paint, line stitches on small patch.

❽ Using handle end of script liner brush and Medium Light Blue paint, place a dot in center left-hand section of large patch. Using handle end of script liner brush and Light Violet-Blue paint, place five dots (arranged as petals) around center dot in this area.

❾ Using Soft White paint, place dots between stitch lines in diamond-shaped area of large patch.

❿ Using Medium Dark Teal paint, place dots in small patch, a dot on hanging thread, and a small dot over center dot in left-hand section of large patch.

Patch—Right Side of Bunny

❶ Using round brush and Medium Light Blue paint, base-paint square patch with two coats.

❷ Using round brush and Light Rose Pink paint, base-paint heart in square patch.

❸ Using script liner brush and Soft White paint, line straight stitches on square patch.

Finishing

Use adhesive/sealant to assemble.

❶ Use a damp cotton swab to remove remaining transfer lines.

❷ Spray all sides of wood with matte spray acrylic finish. Apply three coats, letting each coat dry separately.

❸ Insert a dowel through holes in legs. Slide a spool onto each end of dowels. Slide wheels and candle cups onto each end of dowels. Secure with glue.

❹ Cut ribbon into 18" lengths. Thread both ribbons through loop at top of bell, centering bell on ribbons. Tie a knot to secure bell's placement. Drape ribbons around bunny's neck and tie tails in a bow.

Enlarge pattern 140%.

Stitches the Bunny—Right pattern

Enlarge pattern 130%.

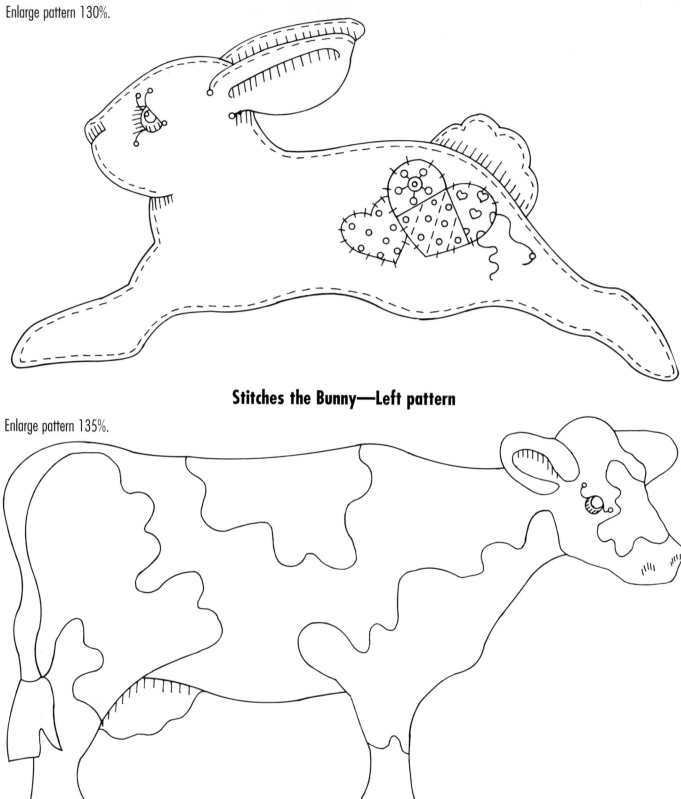

Stitches the Bunny—Left pattern

Enlarge pattern 135%.

Bossie the Cow pattern
Instructions on pg. 42.

b o s s i e t h e
C O W

Designed by Lorna McRoden

Read General Instructions before beginning any project. Trace Bossie the Cow pattern on pg. 42 onto tracing paper, omitting slash marks which indicate shaded areas.

7" x 10" of ¾"-thick clear pine (body)
Two 3¾" lengths of ¼"-dia. wood dowel (axle)
Four ⅝"-high wood spools with ¼"-dia. hole in center (spacers)
Four ⅝"-high wood mini candle cups with ¼"-dia. hole (hubs)
Four 2"-dia. wheels (¼"-dia. hole)
Drill and ¼"-dia. bit
Scroll saw
Stain controller/wood sealer
All-purpose water-base sealer
Oak-colored wood stain
Colored transfer paper
Stylus
Flat brush (#8)
Round brush (#2)
Script liner brush (#10/0)
Clear matte acrylic spray finish
Disposable sponge brushes (1" wide)
1 yd. of ⅛"-wide red satin ribbon
1"-dia. brass bell

Adhesive/sealant
Used sandpaper

Acrylic Paint Palette

Dark Pink
Light Rose Pink
Bright Red
Light Tan
Medium Yellow-Brown
Dove Gray
Very Dark Gray
Black
Soft White

Preparation

❶ Using pattern and scroll saw, cut wood piece. Round edges.
❷ Using drill and bit, drill a hole through base of each leg ¼" from bottom edge.
❸ Prepare wood for staining and painting, referring to Wood Preparation on pg. 8.
❹ Using a disposable brush and stain controller/wood sealer, seal all sides of wheels and spool spacers. Paper-sand when dry.
❺ Using a disposable brush and oak-colored wood stain, stain wheels and spool spacers.

❻ Using a disposable brush, wash all sides of cow with a mixture of ⅓ Soft White paint, ⅓ water, and ⅓ all-purpose water-base sealer. Usually two coats are needed. Let dry. Paper-sand after each coat.
❼ Using a disposable sponge brush and Bright Red paint, paint wheel hubs.
❽ Match traced outline of body design with wood piece. Using stylus and transfer paper, trace design.
❾ Turn tracing paper over so that design is reversed. Retrace design onto other side of body.

When painting dimensional items, paint one side and edges; let dry. Paint remaining side. When painting spots on body, join spots on each side by carrying color across edges. Refer to pattern and photo for placement of shading and details.

Base Coating

❶ Using flat brush and Light Rose Pink paint, base-paint udder.
❷ Using flat brush and Very Dark Gray paint, base-paint spots, ears, hooves, and end of tail.

❸ Using round brush and Light Tan paint, base-paint largest area of eye.

Shading

Use flat brush side loaded with paint for these steps. Refer to pattern for placement.
❶ Using Dark Pink paint, shade top edge of udder and inner area of ear.
❷ Using Medium Yellow-Brown paint, shade lower edge of eye.
❸ Using Dove Gray paint, shade nostril areas.

Lining

Using script liner brush and Black paint, paint line above eye.

Details

❶ Using stylus and Very Dark Gray paint, dot ends of line above eye.
❷ Using round brush and Black paint, paint pupil of eye. Let dry.
❸ Using stylus and Soft White paint, place a small dot at upper edge of pupil.
❹ Repeat for other side of cow.

Finishing

Use adhesive/sealant to assemble.
❶ Using used sandpaper, lightly sand spots on cow to blend brush marks and to create a well-used appearance.
❷ Use a damp cotton swab to remove remaining transfer lines.

❸ Spray all sides of wood pieces with matte spray acrylic finish. Apply three coats, letting each coat dry separately.

❹ Insert a dowel through holes in legs. Slide a spool onto each end of dowels. Slide a wheel and then a candle cup onto each end of dowels. Secure with glue.

❺ Cut ribbon into 18" lengths. Thread ribbons through loop at top of bell, centering bell on ribbons. Tie a knot to secure bell's placement. Tie ribbons around neck in a bow.

Additional Ideas

❤ To make a party animal, give Bossie purple spots instead of black.

❤ Make a small red wagon filled with miniature milk bottles, and hook the wagon behind Bossie. Paint Bossie's wheels to look like chocolate chip cookies. Keep close to the cookie jar.

❤ Use a thimble instead of a bell to hang around Patches the Pig's neck. Or use a miniature spool of thread.

❤ Paint Patches' wheels to look like spools of thread.

patches the pig

Designed by Lorna McRoden

Read General Instructions before beginning any project. Trace Patches the Pig patterns on pg. 46 and 47 onto tracing paper, omitting slash marks which indicate shaded areas.

Specific Materials Needed

7" x 10" of ¾"-thick clear pine (body)
Two 3¾" lengths of ¼"-dia. wood dowel (axle)
Four ⅝"-high wood spools with ¼"-dia. core (spacers)
Four ⅝"-high wood mini candle cups with ¼"-dia. hole (hubs)
Four 2"-dia. wheels (¼"-dia. hole)
Scroll saw
Drill and ¼"-dia. bit
Oak-colored wood stain
Stain controller/wood sealer
All-purpose water-base sealer
Colored transfer paper
Stylus
Disposable sponge brushes (1" wide)
Round brush (#1)
Flat brush (#8 and #12)
Script liner brush (#10/0)
Clear matte spray acrylic finish
1 yd. of ⅛"-wide white satin ribbon

1"-dia. brass bell
Adhesive/sealant

Acrylic Paint Palette

Pale Pink
Dark Pink
Light Rose Pink
Pale Blue
Soft Light Blue
Soft Dark Blue
Medium Light Blue
Medium Blue
Medium Gray-Blue
Medium Dark Blue
Black
Soft White

Preparation

❶ Using pattern and scroll saw, cut wood pieces. Round edges.
❷ Using drill and bit, drill a hole through base of each leg ¼" from bottom edge.
❸ Prepare wood for staining and painting, referring to Wood Preparation on pg. 8.
❹ Using a disposable brush and oak stain, seal and stain all sides of wheels and spool spacers. Paper-sand when dry.

❺ Using a disposable brush, wash all sides of pig with a mixture of ⅓ Pale Pink paint, ⅓ water, and ⅓ all-purpose water-base sealer. Usually two coats are needed. Let dry. Paper-sand after each coat.
❻ Using #12 flat brush and Medium Dark Blue paint, paint wheel hubs.
❼ Match traced outline of Left Side Body Pattern with wood piece. Using stylus and transfer paper, trace design.
❽ Match traced outline of Right Side Body Pattern with wood piece. Using stylus and transfer paper, trace design.
❾ Using stylus and transfer paper, trace tail line onto back edge of body.

When painting dimensional items, paint one side and edges; let dry. Paint remaining side. When painting mouth, join mouth lines on each side by carrying color across front edge. Refer to pattern and photo for placement of shading and details.

Base Coating and Shading

Refer to slash marks on patterns for placement of shading.

❶ Using round brush and Soft Light Blue paint, base-paint eye using two coats. Let dry.
❷ Using round brush and Black paint, paint pupil of eye.
❸ Using #8 flat brush side loaded with Medium Light Blue paint, shade lower edge of eyeball.
❹ Using flat brush side loaded with Light Rose Pink paint, shade half circle in front of eye, under ear, under mouth line, behind front leg, and in front of back leg.

Details

Use script liner brush for steps 2–4 and stylus for steps 1, 5, and 6. Refer to pattern for placement.

❶ Using Soft White paint, place a tiny dot in pupil.
❷ Using Medium Gray-Blue paint, line eyelashes.
❸ Using Dark Pink paint, line mouth, ear, each leg, and feet.
❹ Using Medium Blue paint, paint stitch lines around outside edges of body.
❺ Using Dark Pink paint, place a dot at end of mouth line, ear line, and lines on legs and feet.
❻ Using Medium Gray-Blue paint, place a dot at end of each eyelash and one at back corner of eye.

Repeat all steps in Base Coating and Shading, and Details for other side of pig.

Patches—Left Side of Pig

Use round brush for steps 1–4, script liner brush for steps 5 and 6, and stylus for steps 7 and 8. Use two coats for base painting. Refer to patterns for placement.

❶ Using Medium Dark Blue paint, base-paint small patch.
❷ Using Soft White paint, base-paint all of dotted squares of large patch.
❸ Using Light Rose Pink paint, base-paint remaining squares in large patch.
❹ Using Pale Blue paint, paint a heart in center of small patch.
❺ Using Soft White paint, line straight stitches on small patch.
❻ Using Dark Pink paint, line cross stitches on large patch and line hanging threads.
❼ Using Dark Pink paint, place a dot on lower hanging thread.
❽ Using Medium Gray-Blue paint, place five dots in each white square of large patch.

Tail

❶ Using script liner brush and Dark Pink paint, paint tail line on back edge of pig's body.
❷ Using stylus and Dark Pink paint, place a dot at top of tail.

Patch—Right Side of Pig

❶ Using round brush and Soft Dark Blue paint, base-paint heart patch using two coats.
❷ Using script liner brush and Medium Blue paint, line straight stitches on heart patch.

❸ Using stylus and Black paint, paint dots on heart patch.

Finishing

Use adhesive/sealant to assemble.

❶ Use a damp cotton swab to remove remaining transfer lines.
❷ Spray all sides of wood items with matte spray acrylic finish. Apply three coats, letting each coat dry separately.

Enlarge pattern 165%.

❸ Insert a dowel through holes in legs. Slide a spool onto each end of dowels. Slide wheels and candle cups onto each end of dowels. Secure with glue.
❹ Cut ribbon into 18" lengths. Thread both ribbons through loop at top of bell, centering bell on ribbons. Tie a knot to secure bell's placement. Drape ribbons around neck and tie tails in a bow.

Tail

Patches the Pig—Left pattern

Enlarge pattern 165%.

Patches the Pig—Right pattern

Pattern full size.

Evaporated Milk pattern
Instructions on pg. 51.

Pattern full size.

EAT BEEF!

Chicken Noodle pattern
Instructions on pg. 49.

Patterns full size.

Assembly diagram

Arms
Cut two.

Body

Legs
Cut two.

Diced Carrots patterns
Instructions pg. 50.

chicken noodle

designed by Linda Alexander

These paperweights will give you an opportunity to use the miniature pieces you have collected over the years.

Read General Instructions before beginning any project. Trace Chicken Noodle pattern on pg. 47 onto tracing paper.

Specific Materials Needed

Chicken noodle soup can (10¾ oz.)
2 painted resin chickens (seated 1½" high)*
Small basket of eggs with handle (1" high)*
Small artificial daisies (½" dia.)
Stain controller/wood sealer
Small wood or clay flowerpot (1¼" high)*
3" long x 1" wide piece of balsa wood
Matte knife
One wooden craft stick
Sphagnum moss
Disposable sponge brush (1" wide)
Flat brush (#12)
All-purpose water-base wood sealer
Stain controller/wood sealer
Stylus

Colored transfer paper
Fine-line black ink pen
Clear matte spray acrylic finish
Adhesive/sealant

*These items should be available for purchase at a local crafts store. If not, be creative and find similar items, or mold them out of colored modeling compound.

Acrylic Paint Palette

Dark Peach
Soft White
Black

Preparation

❶ Use stylus and transfer paper to trace outline of pattern onto balsa wood. Use matte knife to cut out.
❷ Prepare wood items for painting, referring to Wood Preparation on pg. 8.
❸ Using matte knife, trim one end of craft stick to a two-sided point, 2½" from one end.
❹ Using disposable sponge brush and oak-colored stain, seal and stain all surfaces of craft stick.

❺ Using flat brush, wash all sides of wood sign with a mixture of ⅓ Soft White paint, ⅓ water, and ⅓ all-purpose water-base sealer. Usually two coats are needed. Let each coat dry separately. Lightly paper-sand after each coat.
❻ Using flat brush, wash all sides of flowerpot with a mixture of ⅓ Dark Peach paint, ⅓ water, and ⅓ all-purpose water-base sealer. Usually two coats are needed. Let each coat dry separately. Lightly paper-sand after each coat.
❼ Using stylus and colored transfer paper, trace lettering onto sign.

Lining

❶ Using fine-line black ink pen, line lettering on sign.
❷ Using stylus and Black paint, dot lettering.

Finishing

Use adhesive/sealant for assembly.
❶ Use a damp cotton swab to remove remaining transfer lines.

❷ Spray all sides of wood items with matte spray acrylic finish. Apply three coats, letting each coat dry separately.
❸ Glue back of sign to craft stick, ½" down from rounded end.
❹ Glue pointed end of craft stick to back of can.
❺ Place a small amount of glue in flowerpot. Cover with moss.
❻ Place a small amount of glue on ends of flower stems, and place them in flowerpot.
❼ Arrange chickens, flowerpot, and egg basket on top of can. Refer to photo for arrangement. Glue all pieces in place.

Additional Ideas

♥ Make or purchase a small witch doll. Make a small sign that says, "Innocent Pie Stander." Glue witch and sign to a large can of pumpkin pie filling.

♥ Paint a small wooden pumpkin like the pumpkin on Miss Kitty's leg. Glue it to a can of pumpkin pie filling.

♥ Make or purchase a small pig or pigs. Make a sign that says, "Ham It Up!" Glue pig(s) and sign to a can of pork and beans.

d i c e d
c a r r o t s

designed by Linda Alexander

Read General Instructions before beginning any project. Trace Diced Carrots patterns on pg. 47 onto tracing paper, omitting slash marks which indicate shaded areas.

Specific Materials Needed

Jar of diced baby food carrots (4½ oz.)
4" sq. of ¼"-thick pine
1 white pom pom (½" dia.)
Orange modeling compound and small sprigs of artificial greenery
Stylus
Colored transfer paper
Scroll saw
Stain controller/wood sealer
Script liner brush (10/0)
Flat brush (#6)
Clear matte spray acrylic finish
Adhesive/sealant

Paint Palette

Pink Acrylic
Medium Pink Acrylic
Light Gray-Blue Acrylic
Medium Yellow-Brown Acrylic
Black Acrylic
Soft White Acrylic
Flat White Spray

Preparation

❶ Use stylus and transfer paper to trace outline of patterns onto wood. Use scroll saw to cut out wood pieces.
❷ Prepare wood items for painting, referring to Wood Preparation on pg. 8. Use Method One to seal wood.
❸ Using Flat White spray paint, paint all sides of wood pieces.
❹ Match traced outline of Body Pattern with wood piece. Using stylus and colored transfer paper, trace head design. Turn tracing paper over so that design is reversed. Retrace onto other side.

When painting dimensional items, paint one side and edges; let dry. Paint remaining side. When painting mouth line, carry color across front edge to other side. Refer to slash marks on pattern for shading.

Shading

Using flat brush and Pink paint, shade inside of ears and across nose.

Eyes

See Tips and Tricks on pg. 9.
❶ Using handle end of script liner brush and Medium Yellow-Brown paint, place a dot for eye. Let dry.
❷ Using stylus and Black paint, place a smaller dot in center of Medium Yellow-Brown dot for pupil. Let dry.
❸ Using stylus and Soft White paint, place a tiny dot in pupil.

Lining

❶ Using script liner brush and Black paint, line lashes and back side of eye.
❷ Using script liner brush and Medium Pink paint, line ear.
❸ Using script liner brush and Light Gray-Blue paint, line mouth.

Details

❶ Using stylus and Black paint, dot ends of eyelashes and back corner of eye.
❷ Using stylus and Light Gray-Blue paint, dot each end of mouth line.

Repeat all steps in Shading, Eyes, Lining, and Details for other side of bunny.

Assembling Bunny

Use a damp cotton swab to remove remaining transfer lines. Use adhesive sealant to assemble. Refer to Assembly Diagram on pg. 47.

Creating Carrots

❶ Use orange modeling compound to mold a carrot ¾" long and ¼" dia. at its widest point.
❷ Using a sewing needle or pin, make a hole in top of carrot to insert greenery. Follow instructions on package for hardening.
❸ Cut a ¾" length of artificial greenery. Using adhesive sealant, secure it in top hole of carrot.
❹ Use orange modeling compound to mold three small carrot tops ¼" long and ¼" dia. Follow steps 2 and 3 to finish.

Finishing

Use adhesive/sealant for assembly.
❶ Spray all sides of bunny with matte spray acrylic finish. Apply three coats, letting each coat dry thoroughly.
❷ Glue pom pom to back side of bunny and full-size carrot between hands of bunny.
❸ Arrange bunny and carrot tops on can. Refer to photo for arrangement. Glue all pieces in place.

e v a p o r a t e d
m i l k

designed by Linda Alexander

Read General Instructions before beginning any project. Trace Evaporated Milk pattern on pg. 47 onto tracing paper.

Specific Materials Needs

Evaporated milk can (5 oz.)
4" sq. of ¼"-thick clear wood
Milk crate with bottles (approx. 1" high)*
Assorted small artificial flowers/ greenery (½" dia.)
Scroll saw
Stylus
Colored transfer paper
Script liner brush (10/0)
Round brush (#2)
Adhesive/sealant
Clear matte spray acrylic finish

*These items should be available for purchase at your local crafts store. If not, be creative and find similar items or mold them out of modeling compound.

Paint Palette

Pale Pink Acrylic
Black Acrylic
Soft White Acrylic
Flat White Spray

Preparation

❶ Use stylus and transfer paper to trace outline of pattern onto wood. Use scroll saw to cut out.
❷ Prepare wood item for painting, referring to Wood Preparation on pg. 8.
❸ Using Flat White Spray, paint all sides of cow.
❹ Center traced design over wood cow. Using stylus and colored transfer paper, trace design onto wood. Turn tracing paper over so that design is reversed. Retrace design onto other side of cow.

When painting dimensional items, paint one side and edges; let dry. Paint remaining side. Refer to pattern and photo for placement.

Base Coating

Use round brush and two coats.
❶ Using Black paint, paint cow spots and cow's head, excluding ears.
❷ Using Pale Pink paint, paint udder.

Details

Refer to Tips and Tricks on pg. 9 and pattern for placement.
❶ Using script liner brush and Black paint, line tip of tail and ears.
❷ Using script liner brush and Soft White paint, line nostril.
❸ Using stylus and Soft White paint, place a dot for an eye.
❹ Using stylus and Black paint, place a tiny dot in eye for pupil.

Repeat steps in Base Coating and Details for other side of cow.

Finishing

Use adhesive/sealant for assembly.
❶ Use a damp cotton swab to remove remaining transfer lines.
❷ Spray all sides of cow with matte spray acrylic finish. Apply three coats, letting each coat dry separately.
❸ Arrange cow, milk crate and bottles, and artificial flowers/ greenery on top of can. Refer to photo for arrangement. Glue all pieces in place.

angel bell
chorus

Designed by Lorna McRoden

These little angels don't sing, but they can make you giggle!

Holy Cow!

Special Materials Needed

2"-high unfinished wooden bell
12mm wood bead
Flat painted resin cow head (1¼"
 high)
5" of ⅜"-dia. black macrame cord
 (tail)
4" sq. of ⅛"-thick balsa wood
15" of ⅛"-dia. white cotton cord
Scroll saw
Colored transfer paper
Stylus
1"-dia. wood ball (udder)
4" of ⅛"-dia. wood dowel (udder)
Wood glue
Stain controller/wood sealer
Script liner brush (#10/0)
Round brush (#1)
Flat brush (#12)
Clear matte spray acrylic finish
Adhesive/sealant
Drill and ⅛"- and ⅜"-dia. bits
8" of ⅛"-wide green satin ribbon
Toothpicks

Paint Palette

Black acrylic paint
Pale Pink acrylic paint
Flat White spray paint
Soft White acrylic paint
Light Gold metallic acrylic paint

Preparation

Refer to Front View of Assembly diagrams on pg. 57.
❶ Using wood glue, attach wood bead to top of bell, aligning holes of each.
❷ Using drill and ⅛"-dia. bit, drill four ¼"-deep holes (in corners of a ⅜"-square pattern) on one side of wood ball. Drill another hole the same size on opposite side of ball.
❸ Using scroll saw, cut four ½"-long pieces from wood dowel. Apply wood glue to one end of each piece. Insert into four holes to create udder. Remaining hole will be used to attach cord to ball.
❹ Using drill and ⅜"-dia. bit, drill a hole on one side of bell, ¼" deep and approximately 1¼" up from bottom rim.
❺ Trace Front and Back Wing patterns onto tracing paper.

❻ Center one of traced wing designs onto balsa wood piece. Using stylus and colored transfer paper, trace outline onto wood. Use scroll saw to cut out wings.
❼ Prepare wood items for painting, referring to Wood Preparation on pg. 8. Use Method One to seal wood.

Painting

❶ Using Flat White spray paint, paint bell inside and out.
❷ Using round brush and Black paint, make three irregular "cow spots," in a random pattern, on outside of bell (use Front View on pg. 57 as a guide).
❸ Using round brush and Pale Pink paint, paint udder.

Balsa Wood Wings

Refer to Tips and Tricks on pg. 9 before beginning.
❶ Using flat brush and Soft White paint, paint all sides of wood wings. Let dry.
❷ Match traced outline of Front Wing pattern with wood piece. Using stylus and colored transfer paper, trace design.

❸ Turn wings over and trace Back Wing Pattern.
❹ Using script liner brush and Light Gold Metallic paint, paint lines on back side of wings.
❺ Using handle end of round brush and Light Gold Metallic paint, make a heart at center, three descending-sized dots at ends of lower lines, and one dot at each point in scalloped lines.
❻ Using round brush and Light Gold Metallic paint, paint a star at end of each upper line. Let dry.
❼ Turn wings over. Using round brush and Light Gold Metallic paint, paint stars on front side of wings. Let dry.

Finishing

Use damp cotton swab to remove remaining transfer lines. Spray all sides of wood items with two coats of clear acrylic finish.

Assembly

Refer to Front and Back Views of Assembly diagrams.
❶ Apply wood glue to each end of white cord. Let dry.
❷ Using a toothpick and adhesive/sealant to secure, insert one end of white cord into remaining hole in udder. Let dry.
❸ Tie a knot in white cord 1½" from ball. Thread remaining end of white cord into bell, going up through holes at top. Using same end, thread cord back through hole at top, going down into bell and leaving a loop at top.
❹ Tie a knot on end of cord. Pull up on loop at top to tighten knot to form a hanger.

❺ Tie two white cords together at top of bell using an overhand knot.

❻ Using black cord, tie a knot ½" from each end.

❼ Using a toothpick and adhesive/sealant to secure, insert one end of black cord into hole on bell. Let dry.

❽ Using adhesive/sealant, glue wings to bell just above black cord tail.

❾ Using adhesive/sealant, glue cow head to opposite side of bell.

❿ Using ribbon, tie a bow. Using adhesive/sealant, glue ribbon in bow to bell under chin.

Ham n' Eggs

2"-high unfinished-wood bell
12mm wood bead
Flat painted resin pig head (1¼")
3" of ⅛"-dia. pink rattail cord (tail)
4" sq. of ⅛"-thick balsa wood
15" of ⅛"-dia. white cotton cord
Scroll saw
Colored transfer paper
Stylus
2 wooden painted Easter eggs (¾" long)
Wood glue
Stain controller/wood sealer
Script liner brush (#10/0)
Round brush (#1)
Flat brush (#12)
Clear matte spray acrylic finish
Adhesive/sealant
Drill and ⅛"-dia. bit
Toothpicks
8" of ⅛"-wide pink satin ribbon

Paint Palette

Flat Pink spray paint
Soft White acrylic
Light Gold Metallic acrylic

Preparation

Refer to Front View of Assembly diagrams on pg. 57.

❶ Using wood glue, attach wood bead to top of bell, aligning holes in each.

❷ Using drill and bit, drill a hole in bell approximately 1¼" up from bottom rim. Drill a hole in top of each egg.

❸ Trace Front and Back Wing patterns onto tracing paper.

❹ Center one of traced wing designs onto balsa wood piece. Using stylus and transfer paper, trace outline onto wood. Use a scroll saw to cut out wings.

❺ Prepare unpainted wood items for painting, referring to Wood Preparation on page 8. Use Method One to seal wood.

Painting

Using Pink spray paint, paint bell inside and out.

Balsa Wood Wings

Refer to Tips and Tricks on pg. 9 before beginning.

❶ Using flat brush and Soft White paint, paint all sides of wood wings. Let dry.

❷ Match traced outline of Front Wing pattern with wood piece. Using stylus and colored transfer paper, trace design.

❸ Turn wings over and trace Back Wing pattern.

❹ Using script liner brush and Light Gold Metallic paint, paint lines on back side of wings.

❺ Using handle end of round brush and Light Gold Metallic paint, make a heart at center, three descending-sized dots at ends of lower lines, and one dot at each point in scalloped lines.

❻ Using round brush and Light Gold Metallic paint, paint a star at end of each upper line. Let dry.

❼ Turn wings over. Using round brush and Light Gold Metallic paint, paint stars on front side of wings. Let dry.

Finishing

Use damp cotton swab to remove remaining transfer lines. Spray all sides of wood items with two coats of clear acrylic finish.

Assembly

Refer to Front and Back Views of Assembly diagrams.

❶ Apply wood glue to each end of white cord. Let dry.

❷ Using cord, make a 2" loop on one end and use an overhand knot to secure loop. Place adhesive/sealant in holes in eggs. Lay bottom of loop over holes. Using a toothpick, push cord into holes. Let dry.

❸ Thread remaining end of white cord into bell, going up through hole at top. Using same end, thread cord back through hole at top, going down into bell and leaving a loop at top. Tie a

knot in this end of white cord. Pull up on loop at top to tighten knot to form a hanger.

❹ Tie two white cords together at top of bell using an overhand knot.

❺ Tie a knot in middle of rattail cord. Apply a small amount of adhesive/sealant to both ends of cord to prevent raveling.

❻ Using toothpick and adhesive/sealant to secure, insert one end of rattail cord into hole in bell. Let dry.

❼ Using adhesive/sealant, glue wings to bell just above tail.

❽ Using adhesive/sealant, glue pig head to opposite side of bell.

❾ Using ribbon, tie a bow. Using adhesive/sealant, glue ribbon in bow to head under chin.

Angel Hare

2"-high unfinished-wood bell
12mm wood bead
Flat painted resin bunny head (1¼")
½"-dia. pom pom (tail)
4" sq. of ⅛"-thick balsa wood
15" of ⅛"-dia. white cotton cord
Scroll saw
Colored transfer paper
Stylus
2 painted resin carrots with wire rings (1½")
Wood glue
Stain controller/wood sealer
Script liner brush (#10/0)
Round brush (#1)
Flat brush (#12)

Clear matte spray acrylic finish
Adhesive/sealant
Needle-nose pliers
8" of ⅛"-wide pale green satin ribbon

Flat White spray paint
Soft White acrylic
Light Gold Metallic acrylic

Preparation

Refer to Front View of Assembly diagrams on pg. 57.

❶ Using wood glue, attach wood bead to top of bell, aligning holes in each.

❷ Trace Front and Back Wing patterns onto tracing paper.

❸ Center one of traced wing designs onto balsa wood piece. Using stylus and transfer paper, trace outline onto wood. Use a scroll saw to cut out wings.

❹ Prepare wood items for painting, referring to Wood Preparation on page 8. Use Method One to seal wood.

Painting

Using Flat White spray paint, paint bell inside and out.

Balsa Wood Wings

Refer to Tips and Tricks on pg. 9 before beginning.

❶ Using flat brush and Soft White paint, paint all sides of wood wings. Let dry.

❷ Match traced outline of Front Wing pattern with wood piece.

Using stylus and colored transfer paper, trace design.

❸ Turn wings over and trace Back Wing pattern.

❹ Using script liner brush and Light Gold Metallic paint, paint lines on back side of wings.

❺ Using handle end of round brush and Light Gold Metallic paint, make a heart at center, three descending-sized dots at ends of lower lines, and one dot at each point in scalloped lines.

❻ Using round brush and Light Gold Metallic paint, paint a star at end of each upper line. Let dry.

❼ Turn wings over. Using round brush and Light Gold Metallic paint, paint stars on front side of wings. Let dry.

Finishing

Use damp cotton swab to remove remaining transfer lines. Spray all sides of wood items with two coats of clear acrylic finish.

Assembly

Refer to Front and Back Views of Assembly diagrams.

❶ Apply wood glue to each end of white cord. Let dry.

❷ Using cord, make a 1½" loop on one end and use an overhand knot to secure loop. Using needle-nose pliers, loosen metal hooks at top of carrots and hook them over bottom of loop. Tighten metal hooks over loop with pliers.

❸ Thread remaining end of cord into bell, going up through hole at top. Using same end, thread cord back through hole at top, going

down into bell and leaving a loop at top. Tie a knot in this end of cord, and pull up on loop at top to tighten knot to form a hanger.

❹ Tie two white cords together at top of bell using an overhand knot.

❺ Using adhesive/sealant to secure, glue pom pom to bell 1¼" up from bottom rim.

❻ Using adhesive/sealant, glue wings to bell just above pom pom.

❼ Using adhesive/sealant, glue bunny head to opposite side of bell.

❽ Using ribbon, tie a bow. Using adhesive/sealant, glue ribbon in bow to head under chin.

Heavenly Ewe

2"-high unfinished-wood bell
12mm wood bead
Flat painted resin sheep head (1¼")
¾" of ⅜"-dia. white chenille stem (tail)
4" sq. of ⅛"-thick balsa wood
15" of ⅛"-dia. white cotton cord
Scroll saw
Colored transfer paper
Stylus
2 wooden hearts approx. ¾" wide (clappers)
Wood glue
Stain controller/wood sealer
Script liner brush (#10/0)
Round brush (#1)
Flat brush (#12)
Clear matte spray acrylic finish
Adhesive/sealant

Drill and ¹⁄₁₆"-dia. bit
Toothpicks
8" of ⅛"-wide blue satin ribbon

Flat White spray paint
Medium Blue acrylic paint
Pale Pink acrylic paint
Soft White acrylic paint
Light Gold Metallic acrylic paint

Preparation

Refer to Front View of Assembly diagrams on pg. 57.

❶ Using wood glue, attach wood bead to top of bell, aligning holes of each.

❷ Using drill and bit, drill a hole in bell approximately 1¼" up from bottom rim and a hole in center top of each heart.

❸ Trace Front and Back Wing patterns on pg. 57 onto tracing paper.

❹ Center one of traced wing designs onto balsa wood piece. Using stylus and colored transfer paper, trace outline onto wood. Use scroll saw to cut out wings.

❺ Prepare unpainted wood items for painting, referring to Wood Preparation on pg. 8. Use Method One to seal wood.

Painting

❶ Using Flat White spray paint, paint bell inside and out.

❷ Using Medium Blue paint, paint one heart.

❸ Using Pale Pink paint, paint remaining heart.

Balsa Wood Wings

Refer to Tips and Tricks on pg. 9 before beginning.

❶ Using flat brush and Soft White paint, paint all sides of wood wings. Let dry.

❷ Match traced outline of Front Wing pattern with wood piece. Using stylus and colored transfer paper, trace design.

❸ Turn wings over and trace Back Wing pattern.

❹ Using script liner brush and Light Gold Metallic paint, paint lines on back side of wings.

❺ Using handle end of round brush and Light Gold Metallic paint, make a heart at center, three descending-sized dots at ends of lower lines, and one dot at each point in scalloped lines.

❻ Using round brush and Light Gold Metallic paint, paint a star at end of each upper line. Let dry.

❼ Turn wings over. Using round brush and Light Gold Metallic paint, paint stars on front side of wings. Let dry.

Finishing

Use damp cotton swab to remove remaining transfer lines. Spray all sides of wood items with two coats of clear acrylic finish.

Assembly

Refer to Front and Back Views of Assembly diagrams.

❶ Apply wood glue to each end of white cord. Let dry.

❷ Using cord, make a 2" loop on one end and use an overhand knot to secure loop. Place adhesive/sealant in holes in hearts. Lay bottom of this loop over holes. Using a toothpick, push cord into holes. Let dry.

❸ Thread remaining end of white cord into bell, going up through hole at top. Using same end, thread cord back through hole at top, going down into bell and leaving a loop at top. Tie a knot in this end of white cord. Pull up on loop at top to tighten knot to form a hanger.

❹ Tie two white cords together at top of bell using an overhand knot.

❺ Using adhesive/sealant to secure, insert one end of chenille stem into hole in bell. Let dry.

❻ Using adhesive/sealant, glue wings to bell just above tail.

❼ Using adhesive/sealant, glue sheep head to opposite side of bell.

❽ Using ribbon, tie a bow. Using adhesive/sealant, glue ribbon in bow to head under chin.

Saint Catopher

Specific Materials Needed

2"-high unfinished-wood bell
12mm wood bead
Flat painted resin cat head (1¼")
¾" of ⅜"-dia. white chenille stem (tail)
4" sq. of ⅛"-thick balsa wood
15" of ⅛"-dia. white cotton cord
Scroll saw
Colored transfer paper
Stylus
18" of ⅛"-wide orchid satin ribbon
1"-high wooden mouse (clapper)
Wood glue
Stain controller/wood sealer
Script liner brush (#10/0)
Round brush (#1)
Flat brush (#12)
Clear matte spray acrylic finish
Adhesive/sealant
Drill and ⅛"-dia. bit
Toothpicks
Needle-nose pliers

Paint Palette

Flat White spray paint
Soft White acrylic paint
Light Gold Metallic acrylic paint

Preparation

Refer to Front View of Assembly diagrams on pg. 57.

❶ Using wood glue, attach wood bead to top of bell, aligning holes.

❷ Using drill and bit, drill a hole in bell approximately 1¼" up from bottom rim.

❸ Trace Front and Back Wing patterns onto tracing paper.

❹ Center one of traced wing designs onto wood piece. Using stylus and colored transfer paper, trace outline onto wood. Use scroll saw to cut out wing.

❺ Prepare wood items for painting, referring to Wood Preparation on page 8. Use Method One to seal wood.

Painting

Using Flat White spray paint, paint bell inside and out.

Balsa Wood Wings

Refer to Tips and Tricks on pg. 9 before beginning.

❶ Using flat brush and Soft White paint, paint all sides of wood wings. Let dry.

❷ Match traced outline of Front Wing pattern with wood piece. Using stylus and colored transfer paper, trace design.

❸ Turn wings over and trace Back Wing pattern.

❹ Using script liner brush and Light Gold Metallic paint, paint lines on back side of wings.

❺ Using handle end of round brush and Light Gold Metallic paint, make a heart at center, three descending-sized dots at ends of lower lines, and one dot at each point in scalloped lines.

❻ Using round brush and Light Gold Metallic paint, paint a star at end of each upper line. Let dry.

❼ Turn wings over. Using round brush and Light Gold Metallic paint, paint stars on front side of wings. Let dry.

Finishing

Use damp cotton swab to remove remaining transfer lines. Spray all sides of wood items with two coats of clear acrylic finish.

Assembly

Refer to Front and Back Views of Assembly diagrams.

❶ Apply wood glue to each end of white cord. Let dry.

❷ Using needle-nose pliers, pull tail from mouse. Using toothpick and adhesive/sealant, push one end of white cord into hole in mouse. Let dry.

❸ Tie a knot in white cord 1½" above mouse.

❹ Thread remaining end of white cord into bell, going up through hole at top. Using same end, thread cord back through hole at top, going down into bell and leaving a loop at top. Tie a knot in this end of white cord, and pull up on loop at top to tighten knot to form a hanger.

❺ Tie two white cords together at top of bell using an overhand knot.

❻ Using adhesive/sealant to secure, insert one end of chenille stem into hole in bell. Let dry. Bend stem into an "L" shape.

❼ Using adhesive/sealant, glue wings to bell just above tail.

❽ Using adhesive/sealant, glue cat head to opposite side of bell.

❾ Using ribbon, tie a bow. Using adhesive/sealant, glue ribbon in bow to head under chin.

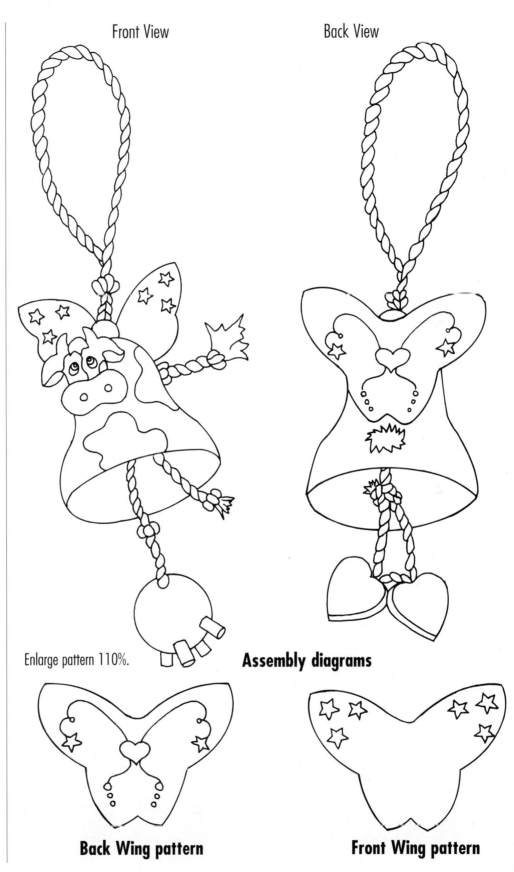

Enlarge pattern 110%.

Assembly diagrams

Back Wing pattern   **Front Wing pattern**

Penny Dolls

During the Victorian era, people handcrafted little wooden dolls for their children, called "penny dolls." Our small dolls were patterned after such dolls and are truly individual works of art. No two dolls will ever be the same, as everyone has his or her own artistic "thumb-print." In other words, no two people will ever paint exactly alike, not even my twin sister and I! So, if your doll looks a bit different than mine, remember that you don't know who is hiding in the piece of wood until you are finished painting! Our dolls were included in this book as an example of face painting. We hope you will be inspired to paint all of the little people and animals that are hiding within you.

dressy betsy

Designed by Lorna McRoden

Read General Instructions before beginning any project. Trace Dressy Betsy patterns on pg. 65 onto tracing paper.

Specific Materials Needed

10" sq. of ¾"-thick clear pine
All-purpose water-base sealer
Stylus
Colored transfer paper
12" of ¾"-wide white twill bias tape
Adhesive/sealant
4" of braided black knit crosheen (hair)
12" of 4mm burgundy silk ribbon
Eight ¾"-long brads or nails
Flow medium
Flat brush (#6)
Round brush (#1 and #2)
Script liner brush (#10/0)
Glaze brush (¾" wide)
Water-base varnish
Scroll saw
Soft lead pencil

Acrylic Paint Palette

Light Peach
Medium Peach
Dark Flesh Tone
Blush
Light Gold
Pale Blue
Medium Blue
Medium Brown
Chocolate Brown
Black
Soft White
Pure White

Preparation—Body

❶ Using stylus, transfer paper, and patterns, trace outline of body and two arms and legs onto wood. Use scroll saw to cut out wood pieces.
❷ Prepare wood for painting, referring to Wood Preparation on pg. 8.
❸ Using flat brush, wash all sides of wood pieces with a mixture of ⅓ Medium Peach paint, ⅓ water, and ⅓ all-purpose water-base sealer. Usually three coats are needed for an even flesh tone. Let each coat dry separately. Lightly paper-sand after each coat.
❹ Match traced outline of Body pattern with wood piece. Using stylus and transfer paper, trace facial features and hair area (omit hair tendrils).

❺ Using pencil, extend lines of hair area around edges and across back of head.
❻ Match traced outline of Leg pattern with wood piece. Using stylus and transfer paper, trace shoe and sock designs (omit dots and vertical scalloped line). Turn tracing paper over so that design is reversed. Retrace design onto front of remaining leg piece.
❼ Using pencil, extend shoe and sock lines around edges and across back of both wood pieces.

When painting dimensional items, paint one side and edges; let dry. Paint remaining sides. Refer to Colored Example on pg. 61, patterns, and photo for placement of details and shading.

Shoes

❶ Using #1 round brush and Black paint, paint all sides of shoe areas. Usually two coats are needed. Let each coat dry separately. Lightly paper-sand between each coat.
❷ Using #1 round brush and Pale Blue paint, paint sock areas.

❸ Using stylus and transfer paper, trace vertical scalloped lines and dots onto front of each shoe area.

❹ Using script liner brush and Soft White paint, paint detail lines on each shoe.

❺ Using stylus and Light Gold paint, place dots on each shoe.

Hair

Using flat brush and Black paint, paint hair area. Usually two coats are needed. Let each coat dry separately. Lightly paper-sand after each coat.

Referring to Layering on pg. 9, layer face with shading and highlighting. Thin paint with flow medium. Let each layer dry separately before proceeding to next step or paint will lift.

Base Coating

Refer to Base on opposite page.
❶ Using #1 round brush and Soft White paint, base-paint "white" areas of eyes.
❷ Using #1 round brush and Pale Blue paint, base-paint irises of eyes.

Shading

Use #1 round brush for steps 2–5. Refer to Shade on opposite page for pat-and-blend technique and placement of shading.
❶ Using script liner brush and Medium Brown paint, reline nose, mouth, line on chin, jaw, and line below eyes.

❷ Using Dark Flesh Tone paint, pat and blend to shade face below eyes, along line on chin, and along jawline.
❸ Using Dark Flesh Tone paint, pat and blend to shade area above each eye and along hairline.
❹ Using Medium Blue paint, pat and blend to shade top edge of irises.
❺ Using Soft White paint, pat and blend to shade bottom edge of irises.

Highlighting

Refer to Highlight on opposite page for placement. Note: After highlighting, you may need to lightly reline along Dark Flesh Tone areas to redefine shading.
❶ Using #2 round brush and Light Peach paint, pat and blend to highlight areas indicated on opposite page.
❷ Using stylus and Black paint, paint pupils in eyes.

Blushing

Use #1 round brush for these steps. Refer to Blush on opposite page for placement.
❶ Using Blush paint, pat and blend cheeks and across bridge of nose.
❷ Using Blush paint, fill in lip areas following lip lines.

White Lighting

Refer to White Lighting on opposite page for placement.
❶ Using #1 round brush and Pure White paint, pat and blend

a vertical line between eyes, and a small area on top of nose, on chin, and on each cheek.
❷ Using stylus and Pure White paint, place a tiny dot in each pupil for highlight.

Details

Use script liner brush. Refer to Details on opposite page for placement.
❶ Using Chocolate Brown paint, outline eyes, line eyelashes, and line eyebrows.
❷ Using Medium Brown paint, reline nose, mouth, and chin.
❸ Using Black paint, redefine hairline and paint hair tendrils on doll's face.
❹ Using Soft White paint, paint a part line in center of hair.

Finishing

❶ Use a damp cotton swab to remove remaining transfer lines.
❷ Using glaze brush, apply three coats of water-base varnish to all sides of wood pieces. Let each coat dry separately.
❸ Cut four 3" lengths of twill tape. Fold each length into a loop. Use adhesive/sealant to glue ends together. Let dry.
❹ Using adhesive/sealant, glue one end of loop to top of each leg and arm piece, and other end of loop to hips and shoulders of doll's body. Let dry. Secure with brads or nails.
❺ Using adhesive/sealant to secure, glue braided crosheen to doll's head for hair.

❻ Make a multibow with burgundy silk ribbon. Using adhesive/sealant to secure, glue bow to doll's hair.
❼ Dress doll as desired.

Additional Ideas

♥ Dress up Dressy Betsy like a storybook, fairy tale, or nursery rhyme character, like Little Bo Peep or Cinderella. Give doll as a present with a book about the character to a special girl for Christmas.

♥ Change Betsy's outfits for the holidays and seasons throughout the year.

♥ Dress Betsy like a country milk maid and keep her in the kitchen for good luck.

♥ Change Betsy's hair and eye color to match another little girl, and give her the doll on a special birthday.

♥ Dress Betsy like an angel. Make a chair that matches Betsy's outfit. Sit Betsy in the chair, and place her on the mantle or another prominent place to keep watch over your family.

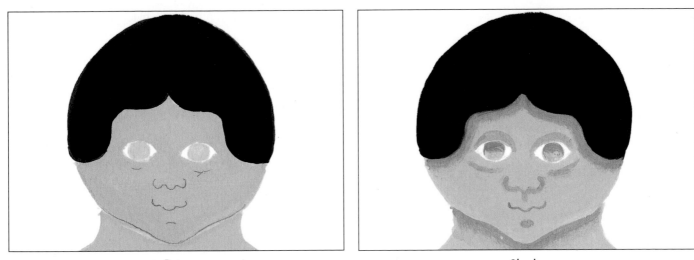

Base

Shade

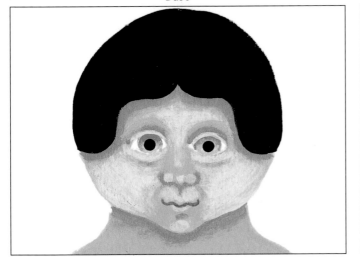

Highlight

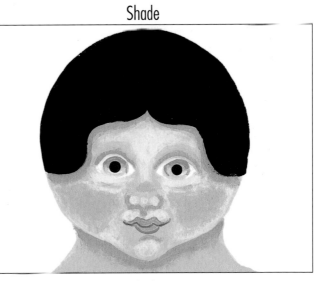

Blush

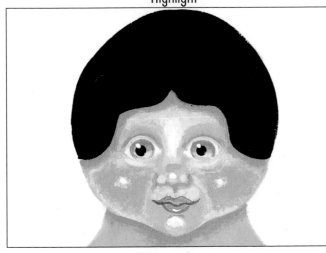

White Lighting

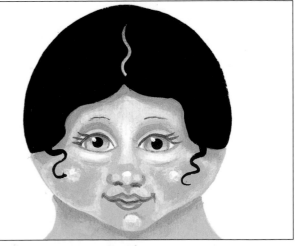

Details

Dressy Betsy Colored Example (face)

joli rabbit

Designed by Linda Alexander

Joli Rabbit is painted in the same manner as Dressy Betsy, using the pat-and-blend method. Refer to pg. 61 for painting technique and shading.

Read General Instructions before beginning any project. Trace Joli Rabbit patterns on pg. 65 onto tracing paper, omitting slash marks which indicate shaded areas.

Specific Materials Needed

10" sq. of ¾"-thick clear pine
All-purpose water-base sealer
Stylus
White and colored transfer paper
One ¾"-dia. white pom-pom (tail)
12" of ¾"-wide white twill bias tape
Eight ¾"-long brads or nails
⅛"- and ¼"-dia. wood dowels (4")
½"-dia. wood disk (¼" thick)
Scroll saw
Flow medium
Round brush (#1 and #2)
Script liner brush (#10/0)
Flat brush (#12)
Glaze brush (¾" wide)
Adhesive/sealant
Water-base varnish
Soft lead pencil

Acrylic Paint Palette

Medium Coral
Light Tan
Medium Yellow-Brown
Dove Gray
Charcoal
Black
Soft White
Pure White

Preparation—Body

❶ Using stylus, transfer paper, and patterns, trace outline of body and two arms and legs onto wood. Use scroll saw to cut out.
❷ Prepare wood for painting, referring to Wood Preparation on pg. 8.
❸ Using flat brush, wash all sides of wood pieces with a mixture of ⅓ Black paint, ⅓ water, and ⅓ all-purpose water-base sealer. Usually three coats are needed for an even color. Let each coat dry separately. Lightly paper-sand after each coat.
❹ Match traced outline of Body pattern with wood piece. Using stylus and white transfer paper, trace head and chest designs (excluding nose, mouth, and chin lines). Trace paw areas onto arms. Extend paw lines around sides onto back of hands.

When painting dimensional items, paint one side and edges; let dry. Paint remaining sides. Refer to Colored Example on pg. 61, patterns, and photo for painting techniques and placement of shading and details.

Referring to Layering on pg. 9, layer face with shading and highlighting. Thin paint with flow medium. Let each layer dry separately before proceeding to next step or paint will lift.

Base Coating

Refer to Base on pg. 61.
❶ Using #2 round brush and Soft White paint, base-paint inside of ears, area on chest, muzzle, and forehead.
❷ Using flat brush and Soft White paint, base-paint paw areas.
❸ Using #1 round brush and Medium Yellow-Brown paint, base-paint lower areas of eyes.
❹ Using stylus and Black paint, paint pupils in eyes.

❺ Match traced outline of Body pattern with wood piece. Using stylus and transfer paper, trace nose, mouth, and chin lines onto white area.
❻ Using #1 round brush and Medium Coral paint, base-paint nose and lower lip.
❼ Using #1 round brush and Charcoal paint, base-paint inside of mouth.

Shading

Refer to Shade on pg. 61 and slash marks on pattern for placement of shading.

Using #1 round brush and Dove Gray paint, shade under chin, along mouth lines, above nose, and at top of white area on forehead.

Highlighting

Use #1 round brush for highlighting in steps 2–3. Refer to Highlight on pg. 61 for pat-and-blend technique and to slash marks on pattern for placement of shading.
❶ Using Dove Gray paint, pat and blend highlights above and below each eye and along top of head in front of each ear. Let dry.
❷ Using Soft White paint, pat and blend highlights on front edge of ears and along line just above eyes.
❸ Using Light Tan paint, pat and blend highlights along lower edge of iris in eyes.

Blushing

Refer to Blush on pg. 61 for pat-and-blend technique.

Using #1 round brush and Medium Coral paint, pat and blend base of inner ears, blending upward into white areas.

White Lighting

Refer to White Lighting on pg. 61 for pat-and-blend technique.

Using #1 round brush and Pure White paint, highlight a small area in Light Tan highlighted areas of each eye and in Medium Coral area at tip of nose.

Details

Use script liner brush for steps 1–3. Refer to Details on pg. 61 and photo for placement. Refer to Tips and Tricks on pg. 9 for dot hearts.

❶ Using Charcoal paint, line lower edge of nose and paint tiny diagonal "fur" lines in white areas on head, chest, and on back of hands.

❷ Using Soft White paint, line above and below eyes.

❸ Using Black paint, paint long "hair" lines inside ears and eyelashes.

❹ Using stylus and Pure White paint, place two dots on each pupil (top dot should be larger than lower).

❺ Using pencil, lightly sketch in paw prints onto edges of arms and feet.

❻ Using ¼"-dia. wood dowel and Medium Coral paint, place a dot heart on each foot and hand.

❼ Using ⅛"-dia. wood dowel and Medium Coral paint, place dots on each foot and hand.

❽ Using script liner brush and Dove Gray paint, paint a line between toes on each paw.

Finishing

❶ Use a damp cotton swab to remove remaining transfer lines.

❷ Using glaze brush, apply three coats of water base varnish to all sides of wood pieces. Let each coat dry separately.

❸ Cut four 3" lengths of twill tape. Fold each length into a loop. Use adhesive/sealant to glue ends together. Let dry.

❹ Using adhesive/sealant, glue one end of loop to top of each leg and arm piece, and other end of loop to hips and shoulders of doll's body. Let dry. Secure with brads or nails.

❺ Using adhesive/sealant to secure, attach disk to back of rabbit for tail base. Attach pom-pom to disk.

❻ Dress doll as desired.

thomas cat

Designed by Linda Alexander

Thomas Cat is painted in the same manner as Dressy Betsy, using the pat-and-blend method. Refer to Colored Example on pg. 61 for painting techniques.

Read General Instructions before beginning any project. Trace Thomas Cat patterns on pg. 65 onto tracing paper, omitting slash marks which indicate shaded areas.

Specific Materials Needed

10" sq. of ¾"-thick clear pine
All-purpose water-base sealer
Stylus
Colored transfer paper
5" twisted length of ⅝"-dia. gray mohair yarn (tail)
12" length of ¾"-wide white twill bias tape
Eight ¾"-long brads or nails
¼"- and ⅛"-dia. wood dowels (4")
Flow medium
Round brush (#1)
Script liner brush (#10/0)
Flat brush (#12)
Glaze brush (¾" wide)
Water-base varnish
Scroll saw
Adhesive/sealant

Acrylic Paint Palette

Medium Coral
Pale Blue
Medium Blue
Dove Gray
Charcoal
Black
Soft White
Pure White

Preparation—Body

❶ Using stylus, transfer paper, and patterns, trace outline of body and two arms and legs onto wood. Use scroll saw to cut out.

❷ Prepare wood for painting, referring to Wood Preparation on pg. 8.

❸ Using glaze brush, wash all sides of wood pieces with a mixture of ⅓ Dove Gray paint, ⅓ water, and ⅓ all-purpose water-base sealer. Usually three coats are needed for an even color. Let each coat dry separately. Lightly paper-sand after each coat.

❹ Match traced outline of Body pattern with wood piece. Using stylus and transfer paper, trace head and chest designs (excluding nose and mouth).

Trace paw areas onto arms. Extend paw lines around sides onto back of hands.

When painting dimensional items, paint one side and edges; let dry. Paint remaining sides. Refer to Colored Example on pg. 61, patterns, and photo for painting techniques and placement of shading and details.

Referring to Layering on pg. 9, layer face with shading and highlighting. Thin paint with flow medium. Let each layer dry separately before proceeding to next step or paint will lift.

Base Coating

Refer to Base on pg. 61 and photo for painting technique.
❶ Using flat brush and Soft White paint, paint inside of ears, and areas of chest, muzzle, forehead, and arm.
❷ Using round brush and Medium Blue paint, paint lower areas of eyes.
❸ Using round brush and Black paint, paint pupils of eyes.
❹ Match traced outline of Body pattern with wood piece. Using stylus and transfer paper, trace nose, mouth, and chin lines onto white area.
❺ Using round brush and Charcoal paint, paint inside of mouth.
❻ Using round brush and Medium Coral paint, paint nose.

Shading

Use round brush for the following steps. Refer to Shade on pg. 61, slash marks on pattern, and Back Shading diagram for placement of shading.
❶ Using Dove Gray paint, shade under chin and mouth and along and under nose.
❷ Using Charcoal paint, shade sides of head and shoulders, around and along white muzzle area, and below and along top edge of ears.
❸ Using Charcoal paint, shade back of head at neckline and ears.

Highlighting

Use round brush for the following steps. Refer to Highlighting on pg. 61 for pat-and-blend paint technique.
❶ Using Soft White paint, pat and blend to highlight front edges of ears and curve above eyes.
❷ Using Pale Blue paint, pat and blend to highlight a small section in lower area of eyes.

Blushing

Refer to Blushing on pg. 61 for pat-and-blend paint technique.
Using round brush and Medium Coral paint, pat and blend inside of ears, starting on outer edge and blending up and inward.

White Lighting

Refer to White Lighting on pg. 61 for pat-and-blend technique.

Using round brush and Pure White paint, shade center of Pale Blue section in lower area of each eye and a small section on tip of nose.

Details

Refer to Tips and Tricks on pg. 9 for dot hearts and to White Lighting on pg. 61 for pat-and-blend technique.
❶ Using script liner brush and Charcoal paint, paint tiny diagonal fur lines along edge of white areas along mouth line, around muzzle, and on forehead where white and gray areas meet.
❷ Using script liner brush and Black paint, line top and bottom edge of each eye, and eyelashes.
❸ Using stylus and Pure White paint, place two dots in each pupil (top dot should be larger than lower dot).
❹ Using ¼"-dia. wood dowel and Medium Coral paint, place a dot heart on each paw (foot). Refer to pattern for placement and to Tips and Tricks on pg. 9.
❺ Using ⅛"-dia. wood dowel and Medium Coral paint, place dots on pads of each paw.
❻ Using script liner brush and Charcoal paint, paint long hair lines in ears and line between toes on each paw.
❼ Using script liner brush and Dove Gray paint, paint three long hair lines in each ear.

Finishing

❶ Use a damp cotton swab to remove remaining transfer lines.

❷ Using glaze brush, apply three coats of water-base varnish to all sides of wood pieces. Let each coat dry separately.
❸ Cut four 3" lengths of twill tape. Fold each length into a loop. Use adhesive/sealant to glue ends together. Let dry.
❹ Using adhesive/sealant, glue one end of loop to top of each leg and arm piece, and other end of loop to hips and shoulders of doll's body. Let dry. Secure with brads or nails.
❺ Using adhesive/sealant to secure, attach mohair to back of cat for tail.
❻ Dress doll as desired.

Additional Ideas

♥ Dress Thomas Cat as Puss n' Boots or the Cat and the Fiddle. Display with a copy of the book or a framed print of the character.

♥ Dress Joli Rabbit as Peter Rabbit or Velveteen Rabbit. Display as above.

♥ Dress Joli Rabbit as the Easter bunny, and make an Easter basket to match.

♥ Pull a Rabbit out of your hat! Dress Joli Rabbit in a magician's costume and glue a wand to her hand. Sit Joli on the rim of a top hat or have her "popping" out of it.

Enlarge patterns 135%.

Enlarge patterns 125%.

Enlarge patterns 135%.

Body

Body

Body

Arm

Arm

Arm

Leg

Leg

Leg

Back Shading

Leg

Arm

Paw Prints

Arm   Leg

Paw Prints

Leg   Arm

Dressy Betsy patterns

Joli Rabbit patterns

Thomas Cat patterns

rose planter

Designed by Linda Alexander

Lorna developed this painting technique and the stylized design of the rose.

Read General Instructions before beginning any project. Trace Rose Planter patterns from pg. 68 onto tracing paper, omitting slash lines which indicate shaded areas.

Preparation

❶ Prepare wood for painting, referring to Wood Preparation on pg. 8.
❷ Using a disposable sponge brush, seal and stain all sides of planter box.
❸ Using a disposable sponge brush, wash front, back, bottom, and sides of box with a mixture of ⅓ Teal Green paint, ⅓ water, and ⅓ all-purpose water-base sealer. Usually two coats are needed. Let each coat dry separately. Lightly paper-sand after each coat.

❹ Using #12 flat brush, wash all sides of bows with a mixture of ⅓ Medium Dark Teal paint, ⅓ water, and ⅓ all-purpose water-base sealer. Usually two coats are needed. Let each coat dry separately. Lightly paper-sand after each coat.
❺ Center traced Rose Design Pattern on front of box. Using stylus and white transfer paper, trace design.

When painting Rose Design Pattern, refer to Colored Example on pg. 68, Rose and Bow Detail patterns, and photo for placement of shading and details.

Lining

Use script liner brush.
❶ Using Dark Yellow-Green paint, line top rosebud stems.
❷ Using Light Yellow-Green paint, line bottom rosebud stems.
❸ Using Pale Green paint, line heart tendrils.

Base Coating

Use round brush.
❶ Using Pale Green paint, base-paint leaves.
❷ Using Light Rose Pink paint, base-paint outside petals of large rose.
❸ Using Light Pink paint, base-paint round central area of large rose and all rosebuds.

Shading

Use #6 flat brush for steps 2–6. Refer to Rose Design pattern for placement.
❶ Match traced outline of rose design with wood piece. Using stylus and white transfer paper, retrace details of round central area, petal lines, and vein lines in leaves.
❷ Using Dark Yellow-Green paint, shade leaves along bottom edges, above midveins, and where they go behind rose.
❸ Using Medium Pink paint, shade outside petals where they meet the round central area and where one petal goes behind another petal.
❹ Using Dark Rose Pink paint, shade top area of rosebuds and along bottom edge of top section in round central area of rose.
❺ Using Light Rose Pink paint, shade along right side of vertical scalloped line (round central area).
❻ Using Pink paint, shade along base of each rosebud.

Highlighting

Using #8 flat brush side loaded with Pure White paint, highlight the following areas. Refer to Rose Detail pattern on right side of page and Colored Example on pg. 83 for scallop stroke, open upside-down U-shaped stroke techniques, and petal placement.

❶ Highlight along top scalloped edges and below midveins of each leaf.

❷ Using scallop stroke, highlight scalloped edges of outer row of petals. Paint from back to front.

❸ Using a scallop stroke, highlight scalloped edges of topmost rose petal.

❹ Using an open upside-down U-shaped stroke, highlight remaining petals in central area of rose.

❺ Using an open upside-down U-shaped stroke, highlight two back petals, two side petals, and front petal on each rosebud.

Details

Refer to Tips and Tricks on pg. 9 and to pattern for placement.

❶ Using script liner brush and Pure White paint, line stamen lines in center of rose and line midveins of leaves.

❷ Using stylus and Pure White paint, place a dot at end of each stamen and place three small dots (in a triangular shape) in Dark Rose Pink shaded area at top of rosebuds.

❸ Using end of wood dowel and Pink paint, place a dot heart at end of each tendril line.

❹ Using stylus and Pale Green paint, place descending-size dots at ends of hearts

❺ Using stylus and Medium Dark Teal paint, place a dot at base of each rosebud.

Bows

Wooden bows come in many shapes, so shading will vary according to shape. Bow Detail pattern illustrates proposed placement of detail lines (heavy lines indicate borders) and shading (slash marks). Use your own discretion when placing details and shading.

❶ Using #12 flat brush side loaded with Teal Green paint, shade bow loops and ribbon tails.

❷ Using script liner brush and Pale Teal paint, line borders on loops, ribbons, and knot.

Finishing

❶ Use a damp cotton swab to remove remaining transfer lines.

❷ Spray all sides of wood items with matte spray acrylic finish. Apply three coats, letting each coat dry separately.

❸ Using adhesive/sealant, attach a bow to each end of planter box.

Enlarge patterns 135%.

Rose Detail pattern   Rose Design pattern

Bow Detail pattern

Bow Colored Example
Rose Planter patterns

s p r i n g
g a r d e n

Designed by Linda Alexander

Read General Instructions before beginning any project. Trace Spring Garden and Plant Pick patterns on pg. 70 onto tracing paper, omitting slash marks which indicate shaded areas.

Specific Materials Needed

Green metal watering can (1 qt.)
Balsa wood (10½" long x 1" wide x ¼" thick)
Scroll saw
Stain controller/wood sealer
Disposable sponge brush (1" wide)
Stylus
White and colored transfer paper
White vinegar
Script liner brush (#10/0)
Round brush (#2)
Flat brush (#6)
¼"-dia. wood dowel (4")
Clear matte spray acrylic finish
1 yd. of 1"-wide wired ribbon
Silk flowers

Acrylic Paint Palette

Light Pink
Pink
Medium Pink
Light Rose Pink
Dark Rose Pink
Pale Green
Light Yellow-Green
Dark Yellow-Green
Medium Yellow-Brown
Light Gray-Blue
Dove Gray
Pure White
Black
Flat White spray paint

Preparation

❶ Using stylus and colored transfer paper, trace outline of bunny onto balsa wood.
❷ Using scroll saw, cut out wood.
❸ Prepare wood for painting, referring to Wood Preparation on pg. 8. Use Method One to seal.
❹ Using Flat White spray paint, spray all sides of wood. Let dry.
❺ Match traced outline of bunny with wood piece. Using stylus and colored transfer paper, trace remainder of design onto wood.
❻ Using white vinegar, wipe off all sides of watering can to prepare it for painting.
❼ Center traced rose design onto side of watering can. Using stylus and white transfer paper, trace design.

Refer to Colored Example on pg. 70, patterns, and photo for placement of details and shading.

Watering Can—Lining

Use script liner brush.
❶ Using Dark Yellow-Green paint, line rosebud stem.
❷ Using Light Yellow-Green paint, line leaf stems above and below large heart.
❸ Using Pink paint, line ribbon tails (below small hearts).
❹ Using Light Pink paint, line ribbon loops.

Base Coating

Use round brush.
❶ Using Pale Green paint, base-paint leaves.
❷ Using Light Pink paint, base-paint rosebud.

Shading

Use flat brush side loaded with paint. Refer to slash marks on pattern for placement.
❶ Using Dark Yellow-Green paint, shade leaves along bottom edges and above midveins.

❷ Using Dark Rose Pink paint, shade top area of rosebud.
❸ Using Pink paint, shade along base of rosebud.

Highlighting

Refer to Colored Example on pg. 70 for scallop technique.
Using flat brush side loaded with Pure White paint, highlight top edge of each leaf with scalloped stroke and below midveins.

Petals

Refer to Colored Example on pg. 70 for petal placement.
Using flat brush side loaded with Pure White paint, highlight two back petals, two side petals, and front petal on rosebud using an open upside-down U-shaped stroke.

Details

Refer to Tips and Tricks on pg. 9 before beginning.
❶ Using script liner brush and Pure White paint, line midvein of each leaf.
❷ Using stylus and Pure White paint, place three tiny dots (in a triangular shape) in Dark Rose Pink area at top of rosebud.
❸ Using end of wood dowel and Pink paint, place a large heart below rosebud where stems cross.
❹ Using handle end of script liner brush and Light Rose Pink paint, place a small heart at end of each ribbon tail.
❺ Using stylus and Pale Green paint, place five descending-sized

dots at ends of small hearts and one dot at end of each stem.

Bunny Plant Pick

❶ Using round brush and Light Pink paint, base-paint nose.
❷ Using handle end of script liner brush and Medium Yellow-Brown paint, place a small dot for each eye.

Shading

Use flat brush side loaded with paint. Refer to slash marks on pattern for placement.
❶ Using Dove Gray paint, shade area below eyes, between ears, under mouth, chin, and feet.
❷ Using Medium Pink paint, shade areas inside ears.

Details

Use script liner brush.
❶ Using Light Gray-Blue paint, line feet, mouth, ears, chin, and top of head. Line hairs above nose and muzzle lines.
❷ Using Black paint, place dots in eyes for pupils.
❸ Using Black paint, line outside of eyes and eyelashes.
❹ Using Pure White paint, place tiny sparkle dots in eyes and a shine dot on nose.

Finishing

❶ Use a damp cotton swab to remove remaining transfer lines.
❷ Spray all sides of plant pick with matte spray acrylic finish.

Apply three coats, letting each coat dry separately.
❸ Using ribbon, tie a multi loop bow. Attach bow to Bunny Plant Pick with wire.
❹ Fill watering can with an assortment of silk flowers. Tuck in Bunny Plant Pick to complete arrangement.

Enlarge Plant Pick pattern 115%. Spring Garden pattern full size.

Spring Garden pattern

Spring Garden Color Example (rosebud)

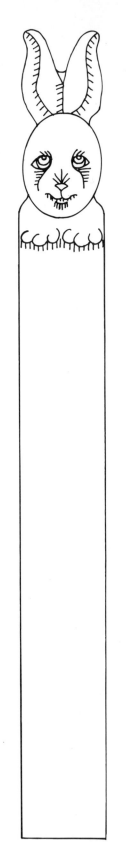

Plant Pick pattern

70

roses &
blueberries

Designed by Lorna McRoden

Grandmas like to keep this stool on hand for their visiting grandchildren.

Read General Instructions before beginning any project. Trace Roses & Blueberries patterns on pg. 73 onto tracing paper, omitting slash marks, which indicate shaded areas.

Specific Materials Needed

Purchased unfinished-wood step stool (two steps)
Stain controller/wood sealer
Oak-colored wood stain
All-purpose water-base sealer
White transfer paper
Stylus
$\frac{1}{8}$"-dia. wood dowel (4")
Disposable sponge brushes (1" and 2" wide)
Round brush (#1)
Flat brush (#8)
Script liner brush (#10/0)
Glaze brush ($\frac{3}{4}$" wide)
Water-base varnish
Clear matte spray acrylic finish

Acrylic Paint Palette

Light Pink
Pink
Light Rose Pink
Dark Rose Pink
Pale Green
Dark Yellow-Green
Pale Blue
Medium Blue
Medium Dark Blue
Dark Blue
Pure White

Preparation

❶ Prepare wood for painting, referring to Wood Preparation on pg. 8.
❷ Using 2"-wide disposable sponge brush, seal and stain all sides of step stool. Paper-sand when dry.
❸ Using 1"-wide disposable sponge brush, wash top of each step and sides with a mixture of $\frac{1}{3}$ Dark Blue paint, $\frac{1}{3}$ water, and $\frac{1}{3}$ all-purpose water-base sealer. Usually two coats are needed. Let each coat dry separately. Lightly paper-sand after each coat.
❹ Place traced outline of Large Motif on top step next to back edge, centering from side to side. Using stylus and white transfer paper, trace design.
❺ Place traced outline of Small Motif on left-hand side of bottom step, centering from top to bottom. Using stylus and white transfer paper, trace design. Turn tracing paper over so that design is reversed. Retrace design onto right-hand side of bottom step.

Refer to Colored Example on opposite page, patterns, and photo for placement of details.

Lining

Use script liner brush.
❶ Using Light Rose Pink paint, line tails of bow on top step.
❷ Using Light Pink paint, line bow loops on top step.
❸ Using Dark Yellow-Green paint, line all stems on both steps.

Base Coating

Use round brush.
❶ Using Pale Green paint, paint rose leaf and small teardrop-shaped leaves on both steps.
❷ Using Light Pink paint, paint rosebuds.
❸ Using Pale Blue paint, paint round blueberries.

Shading

Use flat brush side loaded with paint. Refer to slash lines on patterns for placement.
❶ Using Dark Yellow-Green paint, shade rose leaves along midveins and bottom edges and shade round edge of teardrop-shaped leaves.
❷ Using Pink paint, shade along base of each rosebud.
❸ Using Dark Rose Pink paint, shade top area of each rosebud.
❹ Using Medium Blue paint, shade base of each blueberry.
❺ Using Medium Dark Blue paint, shade dimples of blueberries.

Highlighting

Use flat brush side loaded with Pure White paint. Refer to Colored Example on opposite page for U-shaped stroke technique.
❶ Highlight along unshaded side of midvein and along each unshaded edge of rose leaves.
❷ Highlight two back petals, two side petals, and front petal on each rosebud using an upside-down U-shaped stroke.
❸ Highlight top edges of blueberries (opposite shading).

Details

Refer to Tips and Tricks on pg. 9 and photo for placement. Use stylus for steps 3–8.
❶ Using script liner brush and Pure White paint, place three short lines extending from top of each blueberry.

❷ Using ⅛"-dia. dowel and Pink paint, place a heart at end of each tendril on top step design.

❸ Using Pink paint, place a dot at each point of ribbon tail of top step design.

❹ Using Pale Green paint, place five descending-size dots at end of each heart on top step design.

❺ Using Pale Green paint, place a dot at bottom of each stem on bottom step design.

❻ Using Light Rose Pink paint, place a teardrop at tip of each stem on both steps.

❼ Using Light Pink paint, place a dot at base of each rosebud.

❽ Using Pure White paint, place three tiny dots (in a triangular shape) in Dark Rose Pink-shaded areas of rosebuds.

Finishing

❶ Use a damp cotton swab to remove remaining transfer lines.

❷ Using glaze brush and water-base varnish, apply four coats of varnish to top of each step. Let each coat dry separately.

❸ Spray all sides of wood items with matte spray acrylic finish. Apply three coats, letting each coat dry separately.

Enlarge Small Motif pattern 120%.
Enlarge Large Motif pattern 105%.

Small Motif

Roses & Blueberries Colored Example
(small motif)

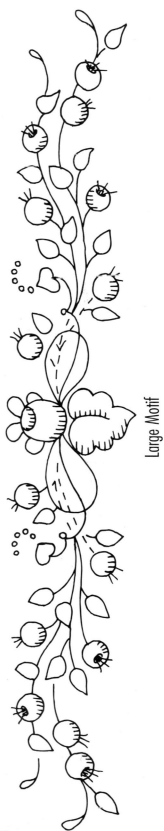

Large Motif

Roses & Blueberries patterns

73

sunflowers & pansies

Designed by Lorna McRoden

Read General Instructions before beginning any project. Trace Sunflowers & Pansies patterns on pg. 76 onto tracing paper, omitting slash marks which indicate shaded areas.

Specific Materials Needed

Unfinished window box (approx. 20" high x 17" wide x 4" deep)
All-purpose water-base sealer
Stylus
White transfer paper
Disposable sponge brush (2" wide)
Round brush (#1)
Flat brush (#6 and #8)
Script liner brush (#10/0)
⅛"- and ¼"-dia. wood dowels (4")
Clear matte spray acrylic finish
Artificial ivy vine with white flowers (3 feet long)
Nine artificial sunflowers (4" dia.)
Nine artificial pansies (2" dia.)
Mixed-annuals seed packet
Wooden craft stick
Artificial bee (1½" long)
Floral foam (to fit box)
Small pkg. sphagnum moss
Hot glue gun and glue sticks
Wire cutters

Acrylic Paint Palette

Light Pink
Light Yellow
Golden Yellow
Pale Green
Dark Yellow-Green
Medium Blue
Medium Dark Blue
Dark Blue
Light Violet-Blue
Violet-Blue
Light Violet
Dark Purple
Light Tan
Chocolate Brown
Black
Soft White
Pure White

Preparation

❶ Prepare wood for painting, referring to Wood Preparation on pg. 8.
❷ Using disposable sponge brush, wash all sides of window box with a mixture of ⅓ Dark Blue paint, ⅓ water, and ⅓ all-purpose water-base sealer. Usually two coats are needed. Let each coat dry separately. Lightly paper-sand after each coat.

❸ Center traced design on front of box area. Using stylus and white transfer paper, trace design.

When painting design, refer to Colored Example on pg. 76, pattern, and photo for placement of shading and details.

Lining

Using script liner bush and Pale Green paint, line all stems and tendrils.

Base Coating

Use round brush for steps 1–6.
❶ Using Pale Green paint, paint all leaves.
❷ Using Violet-Blue paint, paint two back pansy petals, leaving a fine line between areas.
❸ Using Light Violet paint, paint two middle pansy petals.
❹ Using Light Violet-Blue paint, paint front pansy petal.
❺ Using Light Yellow paint, paint sunflower petals.
❻ Using Light Tan paint, paint sunflower centers.
❼ Using ¼"-dia. wood dowel and Medium Blue paint, paint

descending-sized dots on stems for berries.

Shading

Use #8 flat brush side loaded with paint for step 1. Use #6 flat brush side loaded with paint for remaining steps. Refer to slash marks on pattern for placement.
❶ Using Dark Yellow-Green paint, shade above midveins of pansy leaves, along lower scalloped edges, and where leaves go behind pansy.
❷ Using Dark Purple paint, shade two back pansy petals behind middle petals, and where one petal goes behind another.
❸ Using Violet-Blue paint, shade middle pansy petals behind the front petal.
❹ Using Golden Yellow paint, shade bases of sunflower petals.
❺ Using Chocolate Brown paint, shade lower edge of each sunflower center and shade a dip in center of each sunflower.
❻ Using Medium Dark Blue paint, shade edge of each berry.

Highlighting

Refer to Colored Example on pg. 76 and photo for scallop stroke technique and placement.
❶ Using #8 flat brush side loaded with Soft White paint, highlight midveins and unshaded edge of each leaf.
❷ Using #8 flat brush side loaded with Pure White paint, highlight scallop edges of pansy petals using scallop stroke.

❸ Using #8 flat brush side loaded with Pure White paint, highlight tips of sunflower petals, below shading in dip of sunflowers, and on unshaded edges of berries.

Details

Refer to Tips and Tricks on pg. 9 before beginning.

❶ Using script liner brush and Black paint, place accent lines on front petal of pansy.

❷ Using handle end of #6 flat brush and Light Yellow paint, place a dot in center of pansy. Let dry.

❸ Using stylus and Black paint, place a smaller dot in center of Light Yellow dot, pulling it up into a teardrop shape. Let dry.

❹ Using stylus and Pure White paint, place a dot on each side of Black teardrop at its top. Pull each dot out into a teardrop shape following top edge of front petal.

❺ Using ⅛"-dia. dowel and Light Pink paint, place a heart at end of each tendril and above pansy.

❻ Using stylus and Pale Green paint, place five descending-sized dots below hearts at end of each tendril.

❼ Using stylus and Pale Green paint, place a dot at points on each tendril.

Finishing

Refer to photo for placement of flowers.

❶ Use a damp cotton swab to remove remaining transfer lines.

❷ Spray all sides of flowerbox with matte spray acrylic finish. Apply three coats, letting each coat dry separately.

❸ Cut floral foam to fit inside flowerbox. Hot-glue in place.

❹ Hot-glue sphagnum-moss to top of floral foam.

❺ Insert ivy vine into left-hand side of foam. Hot-glue in place. Artfully curl vine around left side of window box frame.

❻ Using wire cutters, cut off three pansy heads. Hot-glue randomly to ivy vine.

❼ Arrange sunflowers around center of box. Hot-glue in place.

❽ Arrange remaining pansies in front of sunflowers. Hot-glue pansies in place.

❾ Hot-glue bee to a sunflower.

❿ Hot-glue back of seed packet to craft stick. Insert into right-hand side of box. Hot-glue in place.

Additional Ideas

🖤 Fill the window box with roses and give as a Mother's Day or Valentine's Day gift.

🖤 Fill basket with fresh vegetables and give to new neighbors to welcome them to the neighborhood.

🖤 Paint window box different colors for different holidays or seasons.

Enlarge pattern 135%.

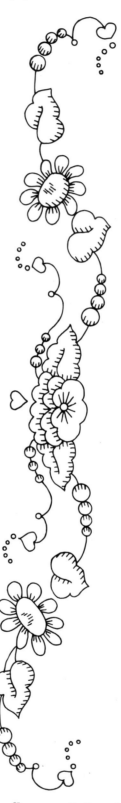

Sunflowers & Pansies pattern

Base Coating

Shading

Highlighting

Details

Sunflowers & Pansies Colored Example (sunflowers)

Lorna's rose

Designed by Lorna McRoden

Lorna developed this painting technique and the stylized design of the rose.

Read General Instructions before beginning any project. Trace Lorna's Rose patterns on pg. 82 onto tracing paper.

Specific Materials Needed

8" x 4" of ¾"-thick clear pine
Two 1"-dia. unfinished-wood knobs
Two #8 brass ceiling hooks (6" long)
One "O" ring hanger
Drill with ⅛"- and ¼"-dia. bits
Scroll saw
All-purpose water-base sealer
Disposable sponge brush (1" wide)
Stylus
Colored transfer paper
Round brush (#2)
Script liner brush (#10/0)
Flat brush (#8)
Clear matte spray acrylic finish
Adhesive/sealant

Acrylic Paint Palette

Light Pink
Medium Pink
Light Rose Pink
Dark Rose Pink
Pale Green
Dark Yellow-Green
Soft White
Pure White

Preparation

❶ Using pattern and scroll saw, cut out wood rose piece.
❷ Using drill and ⅛"-dia. bit, drill two holes ½" deep in bottom edge of wood piece, 1¼" from each end.
❸ If knobs are not pre-drilled, use drill and ¼"-dia. bit to drill a hole ½" deep in each knob.
❹ Prepare wood for painting, referring to Wood Preparation on pg. 8.
❺ Using disposable sponge brush, wash all sides of rose cutout with a mixture of ⅓ Soft White paint, ⅓ water, and ⅓ all-purpose water-base sealer. Usually two coats are needed. Let each coat dry separately. Lightly paper-sand after each coat.
❻ Using disposable sponge brush, wash knobs with a mixture of ⅓ Pale Green paint, ⅓ water, and ⅓ all-purpose water-base sealer.
❼ Match traced outline of Rose pattern with wood piece. Using stylus and colored transfer paper, trace design.

When painting dimensional items, paint one side and edges; let dry. Paint remaining side. Refer to Colored Example on pg. 83, pattern, and photo for placement of details. Slash marks on Rose pattern indicate shading.

Base Coating

Use round brush.
❶ Using Pale Green paint, base-paint leaves.
❷ Using Light Rose Pink paint, base-paint outside petals of rose.
❸ Using Light Pink paint, base-paint round central area of rose.

Shading

Use flat brush and refer to Rose pattern for shading.
❶ Match traced outline of rose design with wood piece. Using pattern, stylus, and colored transfer paper, retrace outline of round central area, petal lines, and vein lines in leaves.
❷ Using Dark Yellow-Green paint, shade leaves along bottom edges, above midveins, and where they go behind rose.
❸ Using Medium Pink paint, shade outside petals where they meet round central area and where one petal goes behind another petal.
❹ Using Dark Rose Pink paint, shade rose along bottom edge of top section in round central area.
❺ Using Light Rose Pink paint, shade along right side of vertical scalloped line in round central area of rose.

Highlighting

Use flat brush side loaded with Pure White paint. Refer to Detail pattern and Colored Example for scalloped stroke technique and petal placement.
❶ Match traced outline of Rose Detail pattern with wood piece. Using pattern, stylus, and colored transfer paper, retrace petal and stamen lines in round central area of rose.
❷ Highlight top edges and below midveins of leaves.
❸ Using a scallop stroke, highlight scalloped edge of topmost rose petal.
❹ Using a scallop stroke, highlight remaining scalloped edges of outer row of petals. Paint from back to front.
❺ Using a scallop stroke, highlight remaining petals on rose.

coat hook

Rose designed by Linda Alexander; Bow designed by Lorna McRoden

Details

Refer to Tips and Tricks on pg. 9 and pattern for placement.

❶ Using script liner brush and Pure White paint, line stamen lines and leaf veins.

❷ Using stylus and Pure White paint, place a small dot at end of each stamen.

Finishing

Use adhesive/sealant to assemble.

❶ Use a damp cotton swab to remove remaining transfer lines.

❷ Spray all sides of wood items with matte spray acrylic finish. Apply three coats, letting each coat dry separately.

❸ Apply adhesive/sealant to threaded end of each hook. Insert into holes in wood piece. Let dry.

❹ Apply glue to remaining end of each hook. Insert them into holes in knobs. Let dry.

❺ Attach "O" ring hanger following manufacturer's directions.

Additional Ideas

❤ For an elegant look, hang a pretty rose-patterned scarf from Lorna's Rose.

❤ Use Lorna's Rose to display pretty hand towels.

❤ Hang roses from Lorna's Rose to dry.

Read General Instructions before beginning any project. Trace Coat Hook patterns on pg. 82 onto tracing paper, omitting slash marks which indicate shaded areas.

Specific Materials Needed

Unfinished 24"-long, 4-peg coat rack

Unfinished three-dimensional wood bow (approx. 1½" wide x 6" long)

Stain controller/wood sealer

Oak-colored wood stain

All-purpose water-base sealer

Disposable sponge brushes (1" and 2" wide)

Stylus

Colored transfer paper

Script liner brushes (#10/0 and #1)

Round brush (#2)

Flat brushes (#6 and #12)

¼"-dia. wood dowel (4")

Clear matte spray acrylic finish

Adhesive/sealant

Acrylic Paint Palette

Pink
Light Pink
Dark Rose Pink
Raspberry Wine
Pale Green
Dark Yellow-Green
Pale Teal
Medium Dark Teal
Teal Green
Pure White

Preparation

❶ Prepare wood for staining and painting, referring to Wood Preparation on pg. 8.

❷ Using 2"-wide disposable sponge brush, stain and seal all surfaces of rack. Let stain dry completely. Lightly paper-sand.

❸ Using 1"-wide disposable sponge brush, wash bow with a mixture of ⅓ Medium Dark Teal paint, ⅓ water, and ⅓ all-purpose water-base sealer. Usually two coats are needed. Let each coat dry completely and lightly paper-sand after each coat.

❹ Using 1"-wide disposable sponge brush and Teal Green paint, paint all outside edges of coat rack and ends of each peg.

❺ Center traced Rose pattern between pegs at each end of rack. Using stylus and transfer paper, trace design.

Refer to Colored Example on pg. 70, Medium Bow detail pattern, patterns, and photo for placement of details and shading.

Lining

Use #10/0 script liner brush.

❶ Using Dark Yellow-Green paint, line rosebud stem.

❷ Using Pale Green paint, line leaf stems and tendrils.

Base Coating

Use round brush and two coats of paint.

❶ Using Light Pink paint, base-paint rosebud.

❷ Using Pale Green paint, base-paint leaves.

Shading

Use #6 flat brush side loaded with paint. Refer to slash marks on pattern for placement.

❶ Using Dark Yellow-Green paint, shade leaves along bottom edges and above midveins.

❷ Using Dark Rose Pink paint, shade top area of rosebud.

❸ Using Pink paint, shade along base of each rosebud.

Highlighting

Refer to Colored Example on pg. 70 for scalloped stroke technique.

Using #6 flat brush side loaded with Pure White paint, highlight top edge of each leaf with scalloped stroke and highlight below midveins.

Petals

Refer to Colored Example for petal placement.

Using #6 flat brush side loaded with Pure White paint, highlight two back petals, two side petals, and front petal on rosebud using an open upside-down U-shaped stroke.

Details

Refer to Tips and Tricks on pg. 9 before beginning.

❶ Using #10/0 script liner brush and Pure White paint, line midvein of each leaf.

❷ Using stylus and Pure White paint, place three tiny dots (in a triangular shape) in Dark Rose Pink area at top of rosebud.

❸ Using end of wood dowel and Dark Rose Pink paint, place a large heart below rosebud where stems cross.

❹ Using handle end of round brush and Raspberry Wine paint, place a heart at end of each tendril line.

❺ Using stylus and Medium Dark Teal paint, place five descending-size dots at ends of small hearts, one dot at base of rosebud and one dot at end of each stem.

Bow

Wooden bows come in many shapes, so shading will vary according to shape. Medium Bow Detail pattern illustrates proposed placement of detail lines (heavy lines indicate borders) and shading (slash marks). Use your own discretion when placing details and shading.

❶ Using #12 flat brush side loaded with Teal Green paint, shade bow loops and ribbon tails.

❷ Using #1 script liner brush and Pale Teal paint, line borders on loops, ribbons, and knot.

Finishing

❶ Use a damp cotton swab to remove remaining transfer lines.

❷ Spray all sides of wood items with matte spray acrylic finish. Apply three coats, letting each coat dry separately.

❸ Using adhesive/sealant, glue bow to center front of rack.

roses &
bows

Designed by Linda & John Alexander

Read General Instructions before beginning any project. Trace Roses & Bows patterns on opposite page onto tracing paper.

Specific Materials Needed

Unfinished-wood switch plate (single or double)

Unfinished-wood bow (Single: 2"- sq. bow. Double: 1⅛"-wide x 4⅛"-long bow)

Stylus

Colored transfer paper

Disposable sponge brushes (1" wide)

All-purpose water-base sealer

Script liner brush (#10/0)

Round brush (#3)

Flat Brush (#8)

Clear matte spray acrylic finish

Adhesive/sealant

Acrylic Paint Palette

Light Pink
Pink
Light Rose Pink
Dark Rose Pink
Pale Green
Dark Yellow-Green
Medium Dark Teal
Teal Green
Soft White
Pure White

Preparation

❶ Prepare wood for painting, referring to Wood Preparation on pg. 8.

❷ Using a disposable sponge brush, wash all sides of switch plates with a mixture of ⅓ Soft White paint, ⅓ water, and ⅓ all-purpose water-base sealer. Usually two coats are needed. Let each coat dry separately. Lightly paper-sand after each coat.

❸ Using a disposable sponge brush, wash all sides of bows with a mixture of ⅓ Light Pink paint, ⅓ water, and ⅓ all-purpose water-base sealer. Usually two coats are needed. Let each coat dry separately. Lightly paper-sand after each coat.

❹ Place Rosebud pattern ⅞" from bottom of switch plate and centered from side to side. Using stylus and transfer paper, trace design onto switch plate.

Refer to Colored Example on pg. 83, pattern, and photo for placement of details.

Lining

Use script liner brush.
❶ Using Dark Yellow-Green paint, line stem of rosebud.
❷ Using Pale Green paint, line heart tendril.

Base Coating

Use round brush and two coats.
❶ Using Teal Green paint, paint recessed edge of switch plate.
❷ Using Pale Green paint, base-paint leaves.
❸ Using Light Pink paint, base-paint rosebud.

Shading

Refer to slash marks on pattern for placement.
❶ Using flat brush side loaded with Dark Yellow-Green paint, shade leaf along bottom edge and along midvein.
❷ Using flat brush side loaded with Pink paint, shade base of rosebud.
❸ Using flat brush side loaded with Dark Rose Pink paint, shade top area of rosebud.

Petals

Refer to Colored Example on pg. 83 for upside-down U-shaped stroke technique and for petal placement.

Using flat brush side loaded with Pure White paint, highlight two back petals, two side petals, and front petal on rosebud using an open upside-down U-shaped stroke.

Highlight

Using flat brush side loaded with Pure White paint, highlight top edge and below midvein of leaf.

Details

Refer to Tips and Tricks on pg. 9 before beginning.
❶ Using script liner brush and Pure White Paint, line midvein of leaf.
❷ Using handle end of round brush and Light Rose Pink paint, place a heart dot at end of tendril.
❸ Using stylus and Medium Dark Teal paint, place a dot at base of stem and rosebud.
❹ Using stylus and Pale Green paint, place five descending-size dots at end of heart.
❺ Using stylus and Pure White paint, place three tiny dots (in a triangular shape) in Dark Rose Pink area at top of rosebud.

Bow

Wooden bows come in many shapes, so shading will vary according to shape. Mini and Small Detail patterns show proposed placement of detail lines (heavy lines indicate borders) and shading (slash marks). Use your own discretion when placing details and shading.
❶ Using flat brush side loaded with Pink paint, shade bow loops and ribbon tails.
❷ Using script liner brush and Pure White paint, line borders on loops, ribbons, and knot.

Finishing

❶ Use a damp cotton swab to remove remaining transfer lines.
❷ Spray all sides of wood using matte spray acrylic finish. Apply three coats, allowing each coat to dry separately.
❸ Using adhesive/sealant, glue bow to switch plate, approximately ½" down from top and centered from side to side.

Enlarge patterns 110%.

Rosebud pattern

Enlarge patterns 105%.

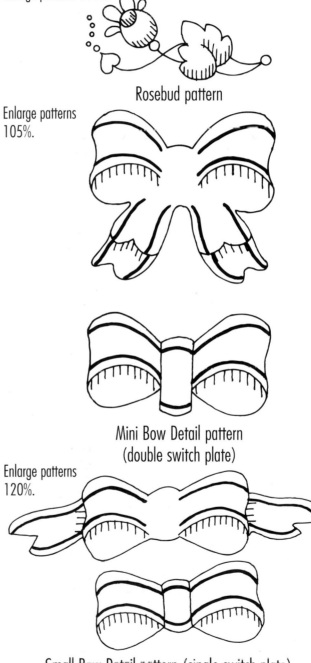

Mini Bow Detail pattern (double switch plate)

Enlarge patterns 120%.

Small Bow Detail pattern (single switch plate)

Roses & Bows patterns

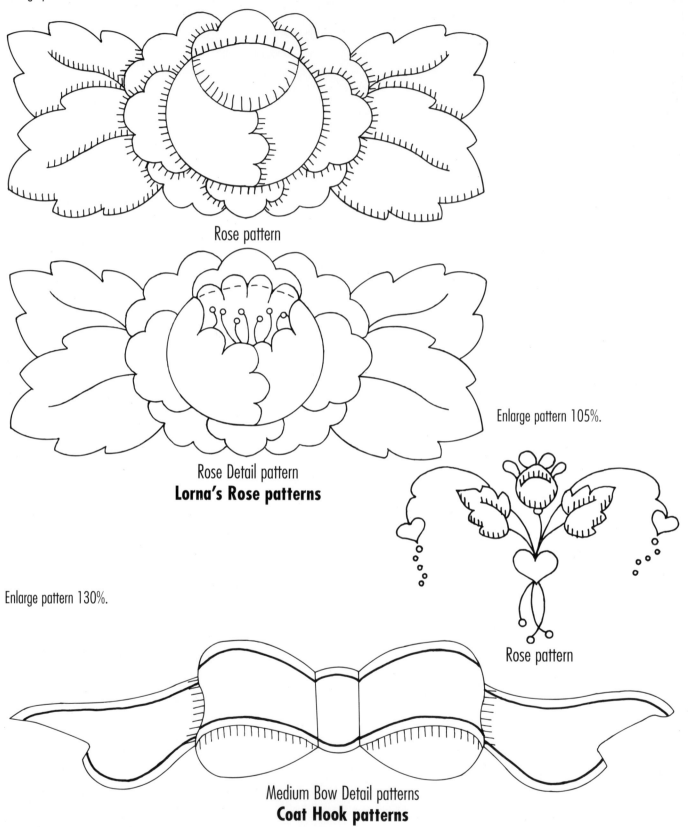

Enlarge patterns 130%.

Rose pattern

Rose Detail pattern
Lorna's Rose patterns

Enlarge pattern 105%.

Rose pattern

Enlarge pattern 130%.

Medium Bow Detail patterns
Coat Hook patterns

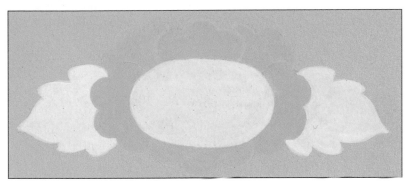

Base Coating

Lining, Base Coating, and Shading

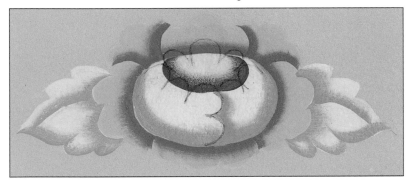

Shading

Highlighting and Petals

Highlighting

Details

Roses & Bows Colored Example (rosebud)

Details

Lorna's Rose Colored Example

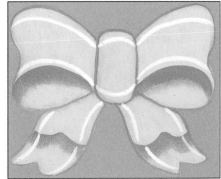

Roses & Bows Colored Example (bow)

raspberry delight

Designed by Linda Alexander

The designs for this birdhouse can be adapted to fit most unfinished birdhouses.

Read General Instructions before beginning any project. Trace Raspberry Delight patterns on pg. 88 onto tracing paper, omitting slash marks which indicate shaded areas.

Unfinished birdhouse (6" wide x 7" high x 8" deep)
Two three-dimensional unfinished-wood bows (approx. 2" sq.)
All-purpose water-base sealer
Stylus
White transfer paper
¼"- and ⅛"-dia. wood dowel (4")
Disposable sponge brushes (1" wide)
Flat brushes (#6, #8, and #12)
Script liner brush (#10/0)
Round brush (#2)
Clear matte spray acrylic finish
Adhesive/sealant

Acrylic Paint Palette

Pink
Light Pink
Medium Pink
Light Rose Pink
Dark Rose Pink
Cranberry
Butter Yellow
Pale Green
Light Yellow-Green
Medium Yellow-Green
Dark Yellow-Green
Pale Teal
Medium Teal
Medium Dark Teal
Teal Green
Medium Yellow-Brown
Pure White

Preparation

❶ Prepare wood for painting, referring to Wood Preparation on pg. 8.
❷ Using a disposable sponge brush, wash front, back, sides, under eaves, and top edge of birdhouse base with a mixture of ⅓ Teal Green paint, ⅓ water, and ⅓ all-purpose water-base sealer. Usually two coats are needed. Let each coat dry separately. Lightly paper-sand after each coat.
❸ Using a disposable sponge brush, wash perch, rooftop and edges, and edges and bottom of birdhouse base with a mixture of ⅓ Pale Teal paint, ⅓ water, and ⅓ all-purpose water-base sealer. Usually two coats arc needed. Let each coat dry separately. Lightly paper-sand after each coat.
❹ Using #12 flat brush, wash all surfaces of two mini bows with a mixture of ⅓ Pale Teal paint, ⅓ water, and ⅓ all-purpose water-base sealer.
❺ Using stylus and transfer paper, trace Roof Motif onto both sides of birdhouse roof (place one motif in each upper corner).
❻ Using stylus and transfer paper, center and trace Front Motif onto front of birdhouse (placement will vary depending upon size of birdhouse).
❼ Using stylus and transfer paper, center and trace Side Motif onto each side of birdhouse.

Refer to Colored Example on pg. 86, patterns, and photo for placement of details and shading.

Lining

Use script liner brush.
❶ Using Dark Yellow-Green paint, line all rosebud and leaf stems and lettering.
❷ Using Medium Dark Teal paint, line raspberry stems and tendrils on roof.

Base Coating

Use round brush and two coats.
❶ Using Medium Yellow-Green paint, paint bottom leaves on birdhouse roof.
❷ Using Pale Green paint, base-paint all remaining leaves.
❸ Using Light Pink paint, base-paint all rosebuds and petals of raspberry flower.
❹ Using Dark Rose Pink paint, base-paint bottom raspberries.
❺ Using Medium Pink paint, base-paint top raspberries.
❻ Using Butter Yellow paint, paint centers of raspberry flowers.

Dotting Raspberries

Use handle end of round brush for steps 1 and 2. Refer to Roof Motif pattern for placement.
❶ Using Medium Pink paint, place dots on bottom raspberries. Let dry.
❷ Using Light Rose Pink paint, place dots on top raspberries. Let dry completely.
❸ Using stylus and Pure White paint, place a tiny highlight dot on each dot.

Shading

Use #6 flat brush side loaded with paint. Refer to slash marks on patterns for placement in steps 1—5.
❶ Using Medium Dark Teal paint, shade bottom raspberry leaves

along edges closest to raspberries and on outer side of midveins.

❷ Using Dark Yellow-Green paint, shade remaining raspberry leaves along top edges and below midveins.

❸ Using Dark Yellow-Green paint, shade rosebud leaves along bottom edges and above midveins.

❹ Using Pink paint, shade base of each rosebud and base of each raspberry flower petal.

❺ Using Dark Rose Pink paint, shade top area of each rosebud and top row of dots on top raspberries.

❻ Using Cranberry paint, shade top row of dots on bottom raspberries.

❼ Using Pale Green paint, shade bottom row of dots on top raspberries.

❽ Using Light Rose Pink paint, shade bottom row of dots on bottom raspberries.

❾ Using Medium Yellow-Brown paint, shade bottom edge of the center of each raspberry flower.

Highlighting

Use #6 flat brush side loaded with Pure White paint. Refer to Colored Example on right of page for scalloped stroke technique.

❶ Highlight top edge of each rosebud leaf with scalloped stroke. Highlight below midveins.

❷ Highlight along bottom edge and above midvein of top raspberry leaves.

❸ Highlight remaining raspberry leaves along edges farthest from raspberries and along midvein.

Petals

Use #6 flat brush side loaded with Pure White paint. Refer to Colored Example on right of page for upside-down U-shaped stroke and for petal placement.

❶ Highlight two back petals, two side petals, and front petal on each rosebud using an open upside-down U-shaped stroke.

❷ Highlight edge of each petal of raspberry flowers.

Details

Refer to Tips and Tricks on pg. 9. Refer to patterns for placement in steps 1, 3, 4, 5, and 7.

❶ Using script liner and Pure White paint, place a line down midvein of each leaf and line side veins of raspberry leaves.

❷ Using stylus and Pure White paint, place three tiny dots (in a triangular shape) in Dark Rose Pink area at top of each rosebud.

❸ Using ¼"-dia. dowel and Pink paint, make a heart on front of birdhouse near peak of roof.

❹ Using ⅛"-dia. dowel and Dark Rose Pink paint, make a heart at end of each tendril on roof.

❺ Using stylus and Light Yellow-Green paint, dot lettering and ends of each rosebud stem, and place a dot at base of each rosebud.

❻ Using stylus and Light Yellow-Green paint, place two dots above and below heart on birdhouse front, and place seven tiny randomly placed dots near base of petals of each raspberry flower.

❼ Using stylus and Medium

Dark Teal paint, place five descending-sized dots at ends of hearts on roof.

Bow

Wooden bows come in many shapes, so shading will vary according to shape. Mini Bow Detail pattern illustrates proposed placement of detail lines (heavy lines indicate borders) and shading (slash marks). Use your own discretion when placing details and shading.

❶ Using #8 flat brush side loaded with Medium Teal paint, shade bow loops and ribbon tails where loops shadow them.

❷ Using script liner brush and Pure White paint, line borders on loops, ribbons, and knot.

Finishing

❶ Use a damp cotton swab to remove remaining transfer lines.

❷ Spray all sides of birdhouse and bows with matte spray acrylic finish. Apply three coats, letting each coat dry separately.

❸ Using adhesive/sealant, glue a wood bow to each side of birdhouse over long stem of rosebud.

Additional Idea

♥ If you plan to use your birdhouse outside, make sure to use a water-resistant, outdoor acrylic finish/sealer.

Base Coating

Dotting Raspberries and Shading

Highlighting and Petals

Details
Raspberry Delight Colored Example (raspberries)

hearts & flowers

Designed by Linda Alexander

Fill this basket with silk flowers, or use it for extra towels in the bath.

Read General Instructions before beginning any project. Trace Hearts & Flowers patterns on pgs. 88 and 89 onto tracing paper, omitting slash marks and broken outline of bow which indicate shaded areas and placement of dimensional bow.

Specific Materials Needed

Two 7" x 9" pieces of ¾"-thick clear pine (hearts)
Unfinished-wood bow (1½" wide x 6" long)
Twelve 3"-long x ¾"-wide x ⅛"-thick clear pine strips
All-purpose water-base sealer
Disposable sponge brush (1" wide)
Stylus
Colored transfer paper
Scroll saw
Script liner brushes (#10/0 and #1)
Finishing nails (1" long)
Round brush (#2)
Flat brushes (#6 and #12)
¼"-dia. wood dowel (4")
Clear matte spray acrylic finish

Assorted greenery and flowers
Adhesive/sealant

Acrylic Paint Palette

Pink
Light Pink
Light Rose Pink
Dark Rose Pink
Pale Green
Light Yellow-Green
Dark Yellow-Green
Teal Green
Pure White
Soft White

Preparation

❶ Using Front and Back pattern and scroll saw, cut wood hearts.
❷ Prepare wood for painting, referring to Wood Preparation on pg. 8.
❸ Using disposable sponge brush, wash all sides of hearts and pine strips with a mixture of ⅓ Teal Green paint, ⅓ water, and ⅓ all-purpose water-base sealer. Usually two coats are needed. Let each coat dry separately. Lightly paper-sand after each coat.
❹ Using disposable sponge brush, wash all sides of bow with a mixture of ⅓ Light Pink paint, ⅓ water, and ⅓ all-purpose water-base sealer. Usually two coats are needed. Let each coat dry separately. Lightly paper-sand after each coat.
❺ Center traced rose design onto front heart. Using stylus and colored transfer paper, trace design.

When painting dimensional items, paint one side and edges; let dry. Paint remaining side. Refer to Colored Example on pg. 70, patterns, Small Bow Detail pattern, and photo for placement of shading and detail lines.

Lining

Use #10/0 script liner brush.
❶ Using Dark Yellow-Green paint, line long rosebud stems.
❷ Using Pale Green paint, line remaining stems and tendrils.

Base Coating

Use round brush and two coats.
❶ Using Pale Green paint, base-paint leaves.
❷ Using Light Pink paint, base-paint three rosebuds.

Shading

Use #6 flat brush. Refer to pattern for placement.
❶ Using Dark Yellow-Green paint, shade leaves along bottom edges and above midveins.
❷ Using Dark Rose Pink paint, shade top area of rosebuds.
❸ Using Pink paint, shade along base of each rosebud.

Highlighting

Refer to Colored Example on pg. 70 for scalloped technique.
Using #6 flat brush and Pure White paint, highlight top edge of each leaf with scalloped stroke. Highlight below midveins.

Petals

Refer to Colored Example on pg. 70 for petal placement.
Using #6 flat brush side loaded with Pure White paint, highlight two back petals, two side petals, and front petal on each rosebud using an open upside-down U-shaped stroke.

Details

Refer to Tips and Tricks on pg. 9 before beginning.
❶ Using #10/0 script liner brush and Pure White paint, line midvein of each leaf.
❷ Using stylus and Pure White paint, place three small dots (in a triangular shape) in dark shaded area at top of each rosebud.
❸ Using end of wood dowel and Pink paint, place a large heart

below center rosebud where stems cross.

❹ Using handle end of #1 script liner brush and Light Rose Pink paint, place a small heart at end of each short tendril line.

❺ Using handle end of #10/0 script liner brush and Teal Green paint, dot ends of all stems and place a dot at base of each rosebud.

Wooden bows come in many shapes, so shading will vary according to shape. Small Bow Detail pattern illustrates proposed placement of detail lines (heavy lines indicate borders) and shading (slash marks). Use your own discretion when placing details and shading.

❶ Using #12 flat brush side loaded with Pink paint, shade bow loops and ribbon tails.

❷ Using #1 script liner brush and Soft White paint, line borders on loops, ribbons, and knot.

Use adhesive/sealant to assemble.

❶ Use a damp cotton swab to remove remaining transfer lines.

❷ Spray all sides of wood items with matte spray acrylic finish. Apply three coats, letting each coat dry separately.

❸ Using glue and nails, join front and back hearts together with wood strips. Starting at bottom point, nail ends of wood strips to edges of hearts. Refer to

Assembly Diagram for placement. Space strips ½" apart.

❹ Center and glue bow to front of basket. Fill basket with flowers.

Enlarge Front Motif and Roof Motif patterns 145%.
Enlarge Side Motif pattern 115%.
Enlarge Mini Bow Detail pattern 120%.

Side Motif

Front Motif

Mini Bow Detail pattern

Roof Motif
Raspberry Delight patterns

Enlarge patterns 145%.

Small Bow Detail pattern
Hearts & Flowers Patterns

Enlarge pattern 195%.

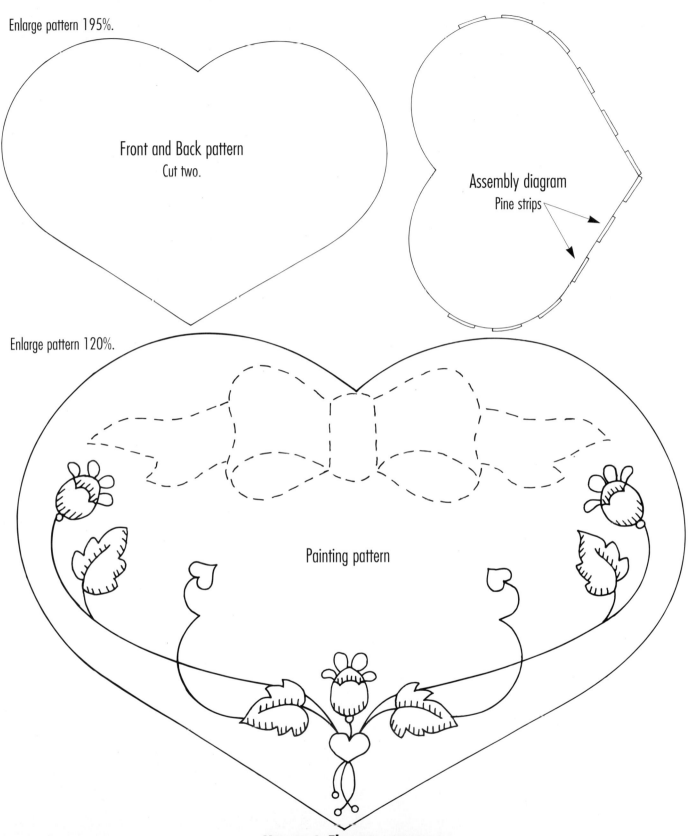

Front and Back pattern
Cut two.

Assembly diagram
Pine strips

Enlarge pattern 120%.

Painting pattern

Hearts & Flowers patterns

t u l i p
t i m e

Designed by Linda Alexander

Read General Instructions before beginning any project. Trace Tulip Time patterns on pg. 93 onto tracing paper, omitting slash marks and heavy lines which indicate shaded areas and accent lines.

14" sq. of ¾"-thick clear pine
Unfinished-wood paper towel pin
   (1¼" dia. x 15" long)
One wood dowel (⁵⁄₁₆" dia. x 9"
   long)
One drywall screw (1¼" long)
Drill and ⅛"- and ⁵⁄₁₆"-dia. bits
Scroll saw
All-purpose water-base sealer
Disposable sponge brush (1"
   wide)
Colored and white transfer paper
Stylus
Script liner brush (#10/0)
Flat brush (#8)
Clear matte spray acrylic finish
Adhesive/sealant

Acrylic Paint Palette

Light Pink
Medium Peach
Dark Peach
Pale Green
Light Yellow-Green
Dark Yellow-Green
Medium Blue
Soft White
Pure White

Preparation

❶ Using scroll saw, cut a 6¾"-dia. circle from pine and round edges on one side (top).
❷ Using pattern and scroll saw, cut out tulip and leaves.
❸ Using drill and ⅛"-dia. bit, drill a ¼"-deep hole in center bottom of base to countersink screw.
❹ Using drill and ⁵⁄₁₆"-dia. bit, drill a ½"-deep hole in bottom of tulip.
❺ Using drill and ⁵⁄₁₆"-dia. bit, drill a hole through center of leaf unit for dowel.
❻ Using drill and ⁵⁄₁₆"-dia. bit, drill a hole in top of base ¼" from edge and ½" deep.
❼ Prepare wood for painting, referring to Wood Preparation on pg. 8.
❽ Use a disposable sponge brush and apply two coats of paint for the following steps. Let each coat dry separately. Paper-sand after each coat.

a Wash all sides of base with a mixture of ⅓ Soft White paint, ⅓ water, and ⅓ all-purpose water-base sealer.
b Wash handle and band around base with thinned Medium Blue paint.
c Wash stem dowel with a mixture of ⅓ Light Yellow-Green paint, ⅓ water, and ⅓ all-purpose water-base sealer.
d Wash all sides of leaves with a mixture of ⅓ Pale Green paint, ⅓ water, and ⅓ all-purpose water-base sealer.
e Wash all sides of tulip with a mixture of ⅓ Light Pink paint, ⅓ water, and ⅓ all-purpose water-base sealer.
❾ Match traced outline of tulip and leaves with wood pieces. Using stylus and transfer paper, trace designs.

When painting dimensional items, paint one side and edges; let dry. Paint remaining side. Refer to patterns and photo for placement of shading and details.

Base Coating and Shading

Refer to slash marks on pattern for placement of shading. Use flat brush side loaded with paint for steps 2–5.
❶ Using a flat brush and Medium Peach paint, paint triangular shaped sections of two outer tulip petals. Apply two coats of paint, letting each coat dry separately.
❷ Using Dark Yellow-Green paint, shade between leaves at bottom and where leaves curl near tips.
❸ Using Dark Peach paint, shade two outer petals of tulip on each side of center petal.
❹ Using Medium Peach paint, shade right side of center petal.
❺ Using Pure White paint, highlight left side of center petal and bottom outer edges of leaves.

Lining

Refer to heavy lines on pattern for placement.
Using script liner and Dark Peach paint, line accent lines on center petal.

Finishing

Use adhesive/sealant to assemble.
❶ Use a damp cotton swab to remove remaining transfer lines.
❷ Spray all sides of items with matte spray acrylic finish. Apply three coats, letting each coat dry separately.
❸ Use screw and glue to secure blunt end of towel pin to center of base.

❹ Apply a small amount of glue to one end of dowel. Insert dowel into hole in top of base.
❺ Slide leaf unit onto dowel. Glue leaf unit to base with design facing outward.
❻ Apply a small amount of glue to end of dowel. Slide tulip onto dowel with design facing outward.

Additional Ideas

♥ You may use the shapés below if you wish to have a different flower. Paint flowers accordingly.

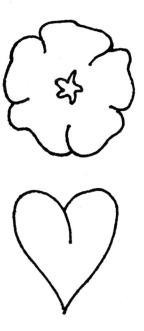

b . a b y
birdhouse

Designed by Linda Alexander

Read General Instructions before beginning any project. Trace Baby Birdhouse patterns on opposite page and pg. 125 onto tracing paper, omitting slash marks which indicate shaded areas.

Specific Materials Needed

4" sq. of ½"-thick clear pine (backboard)
One unfinished-wood birdhouse, (approx. 3" tall x 3½" wide x 1¼" deep)
Drill and ⅜"-dia bit
One dowel (⅜" dia. x 2¾" long)
One "O" ring hanger
Scroll saw
All-purpose water-base sealer
Disposable sponge brush (1" wide)
Colored transfer paper
Stylus
Used toothbrush
Script liner brush (#10/0)
Flat brush (#4)
Round brush (#1)
Clear matte spray acrylic finish
Adhesive/sealant

Acrylic Paint Palette

Light Peach
Medium Peach
Dark Peach
Pale Green
Dark Yellow-Green
Medium Dark Teal
Medium Blue
Pure White
Soft White

Preparation

❶ Using pattern and scroll saw, cut out heart backboard.
❷ Using drill and bit, drill a ¼"-deep hole in center back of birdhouse and in center front of heart backboard.
❸ Prepare wood items for painting, referring to Wood Preparation on pg. 8.
❹ Using disposable sponge brush, wash main body of birdhouse, dowels, and heart backboard with a mixture of ⅓ Soft White paint, ⅓ water, and ⅓ all-purpose water-base sealer. Usually two coats are needed. Let each coat dry separately. Lightly paper-sand after each coat.

❺ Using toothbrush and Medium Blue Paint, spatter-paint white area of birdhouse. Refer to Backgrounds (Spattered) on pg. 8.
❻ Using disposable sponge brush, wash birdhouse roof, landing pad, entry hole, and perch with a mixture of ⅓ Medium Blue paint, ⅓ water, and ⅓ all-purpose water-base sealer. Usually two coats are needed. Let each coat dry separately. Lightly paper-sand after each coat.
❼ Match outline of design with wood piece. Using stylus and transfer paper, trace design onto front of birdhouse.

When painting dimensional items, paint one side and edges; let dry. Paint remaining sides. Refer to Colored Example on pg. 70, pattern, and photo for placement of shading and details.

Lining

Using script liner brush and Dark Yellow-Green paint, line stems of rosebuds and leaves.

Base Coating

Use round brush.
❶ Using Pale Green paint, base-paint leaves with two coats.
❷ Using Light Peach paint, base-paint two rosebuds.

Shading

Use flat brush side loaded with paint for the following steps.
❶ Using Dark Yellow-Green paint, shade each leaf along bottom edges.
❷ Using Medium Peach paint, shade base of each rosebud.
❸ Using Dark Peach paint, shade top area of each rosebud using an open U-shaped stroke.

Scalloped Petals

Refer to Colored Example on pg. 70 for scalloped petal technique and petal placement.

Using flat brush side loaded with Pure White paint, highlight two back petals, two side petals, and front petal on each rosebud using an open upside-down U-shaped stroke.

Details

Use stylus. Read Tips and Tricks on pg. 9 before beginning.
❶ Using Medium Peach paint, place a heart near peak of roof.
❷ Using Dark Peach paint, place a heart at end of each stem.
❸ Using Pure White paint, place three tiny dots (in a triangular-shaped pattern) in Dark Peach areas of buds.

❹ Using Medium Dark Teal paint, place a dot at base of each rosebud on stem.
❺ Using Dark Yellow-Green paint, place a dot above and two descending-sized dots below heart near peak of roof.

Finishing

Use adhesive/sealant to assemble.
❶ Use a damp cotton swab to remove remaining transfer lines.
❷ Spray all sides of items with matte spray acrylic finish. Apply three coats, letting each coat dry separately.
❸ Apply glue to each end of dowel. Insert one end into hole in heart backboard and other end into hole in back of birdhouse.
❹ Attach "O" ring hanger to back of backboard to hang.

Enlarge Tulip pattern 190%.
Enlarge Leaves pattern 120%.

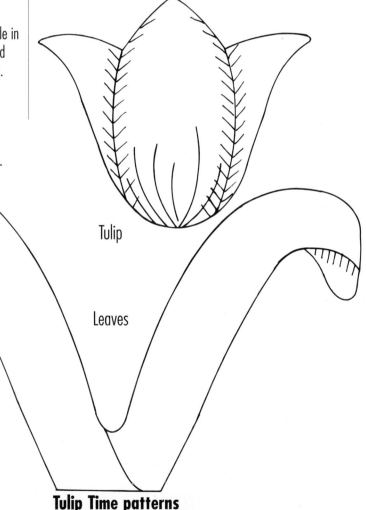

Baby Birdhouse pattern (Backboard pattern on pg. 125)

Tulip

Leaves

Tulip Time patterns

s.h y e s t
v l o l e t S

Designed by Linda Alexander

This necklace is painted in a similar manner as the violets in Colored Example on pg. 97. let it inspire you to use your own creative abilities to create new projects!

Read General Instructions before beginning any project.

1⅛"-high x 1¼"-wide x ½"-thick heart bead
Two 18mm wooden beads
Four 12mm wooden beads
1 yd. of black rattail cording
All-purpose water-base sealer
Stylus
White transfer paper or white chalk pencil
Flat brushes (#2 and #12)
Script liner brush (10/0)
Round brush (#001)
Glaze brush (¾" wide)
Water-base varnish
Round toothpicks

Acrylic Paint Palette

Golden Yellow
Pale Green
Medium Yellow-Green
Dark Yellow-Green
Pale Blue
Dark Blue
Light Violet-Blue
Light Violet
Light Purple
Black
Soft White

Preparation

❶ Prepare wood for painting, referring to Wood Preparation on pg. 8.
❷ Using #12 flat brush, wash all of wood pieces with a mixture of ⅓ Dark Blue paint, ⅓ water, and ⅓ all-purpose water-base sealer. Usually three coats are needed for an even color. Let each coat dry separately. Lightly paper-sand after each coat. Set two 12mm beads aside.
❸ If you wish to transfer designs onto beads, first trace Transfer patterns on pg. 97 onto tracing paper. Center design on appropriately sized bead. Using stylus and white transfer paper, trace design. Repeat this step for all five beads. If you prefer, use a white chalk pencil to sketch outline of color areas onto each bead.

Refer to Colored Example on pg. 97 and photo for painting techniques and appropriate enlarged diagrams for color placement. Paint heart bead first and then descending-sized beads.

Base Coating

Use #001 round brush for the following areas.
❶ Using Medium Yellow-Green paint, paint leaves on bead labeled "B" on enlarged diagram.
❷ Using Pale Green paint, paint leaves on bead labeled "V" on enlarged diagram.
❸ Using Dark Yellow-Green paint, paint leaves on bead labeled "Z" on enlarged diagram.
❹ Using Light Violet-Blue paint, paint five violet petals on bead.

Shading

Use #2 flat brush side loaded with paint. Refer to enlarged diagrams for placement.
❶ Using Light Purple paint, shade left edge of top left petal, left edge of bottom petal, and bottom edge of right middle petal.

❷ Using Light Violet paint, shade left side of top right petal and bottom edge of left middle petal.

Highlighting

Using #2 flat brush side loaded with Pale Blue paint, highlight unshaded edges of two top petals and bottom petal.

Details

Refer to appropriate-sized enlarged diagrams for placement.
❶ Using stylus and Golden Yellow paint, place a dot in upper one-third of bottom petal. Pull dot up into a teardrop shape, stopping where all petals meet. Let dry.
❷ Using a toothpick and Black paint, place a smaller dot on top of yellow dot. Pull it up into a teardrop shape, stopping as before. A small amount of yellow will show around black teardrop.
❸ Using a script liner brush and Pale Green paint, line stems and vein lines on violet leaves.
❹ Using script liner brush and Black paint, paint accent lines on middle petals and front petal.
❺ Using stylus and Soft White paint, place a tiny dot on each side of yellow teardrop, as indicated on enlarged diagrams. Pull these dots up into center, creating a teardrop shape.
❻ Using stylus and Pale Blue paint, paint comma shapes between leaves at top of heart bead.
❼ Using a toothpick and Soft White paint, place descending-sized dots on heart bead only as

indicated on enlarged diagram by open dots.

Repeat steps in Base Coating, Shading, Highlighting, and Details for remaining beads, omitting comma shapes and descending-sized dots.

❶ Use a damp cotton swab to remove remaining transfer lines.
❷ Using glaze brush, apply three coats of water-base varnish to all sides of wood pieces. Let each coat dry separately.
❸ Slide and center heart bead onto rattail cord. Tie an overhand knot on each side of bead to secure in place.
❹ Slide an 18mm bead onto each end of cord next to knots. Tie an overhand knot to secure.
❺ Slide a decorated 12mm bead onto each end of rattail cord next to knots. Tie an overhand knot to secure.
❻ Tie an overhand knot 2" from each end of rattail cord. Slide remaining beads onto cord. Tie a knot in ends of cord to secure.

Additional Ideas

Use the same designs to create matching earrings or a pin.

❤ String beads on a different color cord or a bandanna.

meadow sWeet

Designed by Linda & John Alexander

Read General Instructions before beginning any project. Trace Meadow Sweet patterns on opposite page onto tracing paper, omitting slash marks which indicate shaded areas.

Specific Materials Needed

Unfinished-wood double switch plate
Unfinished-wood bow (1⅛" wide x 4⅛" long)
All-purpose water-base sealer
Stylus
Colored transfer paper
Disposable sponge brushes (1" wide)
Script liner brush (#10/0)
Round brush (#3)
Flat Brush (#8)
Clear matte spray acrylic finish
Adhesive/sealant

Acrylic Paint Palette

Creamy Yellow
Pale Green
Medium Yellow-Green
Dark Yellow-Green
Soft Light Blue
Medium Light Blue
Teal Green

Light Violet-Blue
Light Violet
Black
Soft White
Pure White

Preparation

❶ Prepare wood for painting, referring to Wood Preparation on pg. 8.
❷ Using a disposable sponge brush, wash all sides of switch plate with a mixture of ⅓ Soft White paint, ⅓ water, and ⅓ all-purpose water-base sealer. Usually two coats are needed. Let each coat dry separately. Lightly paper-sand after each coat.
❸ Using a disposable sponge brush, wash all sides of bow with a mixture of ⅓ Soft Light Blue paint, ⅓ water, and ⅓ all-purpose water-base sealer. Usually two coats are needed. Let each coat dry separately. Lightly paper-sand after each coat.
❹ Place Violet pattern ⅞" from bottom of switch plate and centered from side to side. Using stylus and colored transfer paper, trace design onto switch plate.

Refer to Colored Example on opposite page, pattern, and photo for placement of details and shading.

Lining

Use script liner brush.
❶ Using Pale Green paint, line heart tendril.
❷ Using Medium Yellow-Green paint, line stem of violet.

Base Coating

Use round brush and two coats to base-paint.
❶ Using Pale Green paint, base-paint leaves.
❷ Using Light Violet-Blue paint, base-paint all petals of violet, leaving a fine separation line between areas.
❸ Using Teal Green paint, paint recessed edge of switch plate.

Shading

Refer to slash marks on pattern for placement.
❶ Using flat brush side loaded with Dark Yellow-Green paint, shade along bottom edge and along midvein of leaf.

❷ Using flat brush side loaded with Light Violet paint, shade inside edges of two top petals, shade top edge of each side petal, and shade top edge of front petal.

Highlighting

Refer to Colored Example on right side of page for scallop stroke technique.
❶ Using flat brush side loaded with Pure White paint, highlight scalloped edge of two top and two side petals, and across bottom edge of front petal.
❷ Using flat brush side loaded with Pure White paint, highlight leaf below midvein and along the top edge.
❸ Using script liner brush and Pure White paint, line midvein of leaf.

Details

Refer to Tips and Tricks on pg. 9 before beginning.
❶ Using handle end of script liner brush and Creamy Yellow paint, place a dot at top of front pansy petal. Using script liner brush, pull dot up into a teardrop shape. Let dry.
❷ Using stylus and Black paint, place a smaller dot on top of Creamy Yellow dot. Pull dot up into a teardrop shape. Let dry.
❸ Using stylus and Pure White paint, place a dot on each side of Black teardrop at its top. Pull each dot down and out (approx. ¼"), following curve of top edge of front petal.

❹ Using handle end of round brush and Light Violet-Blue paint, place a heart dot at end of tendril.
❺ Using stylus and Teal Green paint, place five descending-size dots at end of heart.
❻ Using stylus and Medium Yellow-Green paint, place a dot at end of tendril/stem.

Bow

Wooden bows come in many shapes, so shading will vary according to shape. Small Bow Detail pattern illustrates proposed placement of detail lines (heavy lines indicate borders) and shading (slash marks). Use your own discretion when placing details and shading.
❶ Using flat brush side loaded with Medium Light Blue paint, shade bow loops and ribbon tails.
❷ Using script liner brush and Pure White paint, line borders on loops, ribbons, and knot.

Finishing

❶ Use a damp cotton swab to remove remaining transfer lines.
❷ Spray all sides of wood using matte spray acrylic finish. Apply three coats, allowing each coat to dry separately.
❸ Using adhesive/sealant, glue bow to switch plate, approximately ½" down from top and centered from side to side.

Transfer patterns full size.

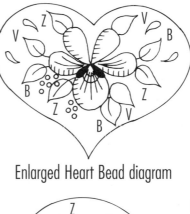

Enlarged Heart Bead diagram

Enlarged 12mm Bead diagram

Enlarged 18mm Bead diagram

Shyest Violets transfer patterns

Lining and Base Coating

Shading, Highlighting, and Details

Meadow Sweet Colored Example (violets)

Enlarge pattern 105%.

Enlarge pattern 110%.

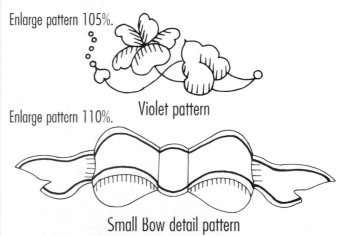

Violet pattern

Small Bow detail pattern
Meadow Sweet patterns

Linda's pansy

Designed by Linda Alexander

Linda developed this pansy using Lorna's scallop stroke technique.

Read General Instructions before beginning any project. Trace Linda's Pansy pattern on pg. 102 onto tracing paper, omitting slash marks which indicate shaded areas.

Specific Materials Needed

4" x 8" of ¾"-thick clear pine
Two 1"-dia. unfinished-wood
 knobs
Two #8 brass ceiling hooks
 (6" long)
One "O" ring hanger
Drill and ⅛"- and ¼"-dia. bits
Scroll saw
All-purpose water-base sealer
Disposable sponge brush (1"
 wide)
Stylus
Colored transfer paper
Round brush (#2)
Flat brush (#8)
¼"-dia. wood dowel (4")
Script liner brush (#10/0)
Clear matte spray acrylic finish
Adhesive/sealant

Acrylic Paint Palette

Golden Yellow
Dark Yellow-Green
Pale Green
Violet-Blue
Light Periwinkle Blue
Light Violet-Blue
Black
Soft White
Pure White

Preparation

❶ Using pattern and scroll saw, cut out wood piece.
❷ Using drill and ⅛"-dia. bit, drill two ½"-deep holes in bottom edge of wood piece, 1¼" from each end.
❸ If knob is not pre-drilled, use drill and ¼"-dia. bit to drill a ½"-deep hole in each knob.
❹ Prepare wood for painting, referring to Wood Preparation on pg. 8.
❺ Using disposable sponge brush, wash all sides of pansy cutout with a mixture of ⅓ Soft White paint, ⅓ water, and ⅓ all-purpose water-base sealer. Usually two coats are needed. Let

each coat dry separately. Lightly paper-sand after each coat.
❻ Using disposable sponge brush, wash knobs with a mixture of ⅓ Pale Green paint, ⅓ water, and ⅓ all-purpose water-base sealer.
❼ Match traced outline of pansy design with wood piece. Using stylus and colored transfer paper, trace lines of pansy and leaves.

When painting dimensional items, paint one side and edges; let dry. Paint remaining side. Refer to Colored Example on pg. 103, pattern, and photo for placement of details.

Base Coating

Use round brush.
❶ Using Pale Green paint, base-paint leaves.
❷ Using Light Violet-Blue paint, base-paint pansy petals.

Shading

Use a flat brush side loaded with paint.
❶ Match traced outline of pansy design with wood piece. Using

pattern, stylus, and colored transfer paper, retrace petal outlines, teardrop area, and accent lines onto pansy; then trace vein lines onto leaves.
❷ Using Dark Yellow-Green paint, shade leaves along bottom edges, above midveins, and where they go behind a petal.
❸ Using Violet-Blue paint, shade two back petals behind middle petals and where back petal goes behind the another.
❹ Using Light Periwinkle Blue paint, shade behind front petal and along lines in front petal.

Accents

Refer to Tips and Tricks on pg. 9 before beginning.
❶ Using end of dowel and Golden Yellow paint, place a large dot in center area of pansy. Using stylus, pull dot up into a teardrop shape. Let dry.
❷ Using handle end of round brush and Black paint, place a smaller dot in center of yellow area. Using stylus, pull dot upward into a teardrop shape.
❸ Using liner brush and Black paint, line pansy accent lines.

Highlighting

Use flat brush and Pure White paint. Refer to Colored Example on pg. 103 for scalloped stroke technique and for placement.
❶ Using scallop stroke, highlight top edges and midveins of leaves, and edges of pansy petals.
❷ Using stylus, place a dot on each side of Black teardrop at its

top. Pull each dot down and out approximately ½", following top edge of front petal.

Finishing

Use adhesive/sealant to assemble.

❶ Use a damp cotton swab to remove remaining transfer lines.

❷ Spray all sides of wood items with matte spray acrylic finish. Apply three coats, letting each coat dry separately.

❸ Apply glue to threaded end of each hook. Insert hooks into holes in wood piece. Let dry.

❹ Apply glue to remaining end of each hook and insert knobs. Let dry.

❺ Attach "O" ring hanger following manufacturer's directions.

Additional Ideas

❤ Make a series of several different colored pansies, and hang them in your entryway for guests and family members to hang their jackets.

❤ Use eye hooks and chain instead of ceiling hooks. Hang a sign with your family name or house number from pansy. Seal with a water-resistant, outdoor finish/sealer. Hang outside your front door.

p a n s y
c l o c k

Clock designed by Linda Alexander; Bow designed by Lorna McRoden

This pansy is a reminder of spring throughout the year.

Read General Instructions before beginning any project. Trace Pansy Clock patterns on pgs. 102 and 103 onto tracing paper, omitting slash marks which indicate shaded areas.

Specific Materials Needed

7" x 10" of ¾"-thick clear pine (clock)
Unfinished three-dimensional bow (2" high x 9½" long)
Clockwork
Two 2" lengths of ¼"-wide brass chain
Four brass eye hooks, ¼" dia.
One "O" ring hanger
Drill and ⁵⁄₁₆"-dia. bit
Scroll saw
All-purpose water-base sealer
Disposable sponge brush (2" wide)
White and colored transfer paper
Stylus
Round brush (#1)
Flat brush (#8)
Script liner brushes (#1 and #10/0)
Water-base varnish
Glaze brush (¾" wide)

One AA battery
Needle-nose pliers
Adhesive/sealant

Acrylic Paint Palette

Pale Pink
Butter Yellow
Pale Green
Dark Yellow-Green
Pale Blue
Medium Blue
Light Violet-Blue
Lilac
Light Purple
Dark Purple
Black
Pure White
Soft White

Preparation

❶ Using pattern and scroll saw, cut out clock wood piece.

❷ Using drill and ⁵⁄₁₆"-dia. bit, drill hole in center of clock piece, as indicated on pattern.

❸ Prepare wood items for painting, referring to Wood Preparation on pg. 8.

❹ Using disposable sponge brush, wash all sides of clock with a mixture of ⅓ Soft White paint, ⅓ water, and ⅓ all-purpose water-base sealer. Usually two coats are needed. Let each coat dry separately. Lightly paper-sand after each coat.

❺ Using disposable sponge brush, wash all sides of bow with a mixture of ⅓ Pale Blue paint, ⅓ water, and ⅓ all-purpose water-base sealer. Usually two coats are needed. Let each coat dry separately. Lightly paper-sand after each coat.

❻ Match traced outline of clock design with wood piece. Using stylus and colored transfer paper, trace design onto clock face, excluding accent lines and dots that indicate clock positions on pansy. *Note: Bow design is not traced on wood pieces.*

❼ Using flat brush and Medium Blue paint, paint outer edge of heart clock.

Refer to Colored Example on pg. 103, patterns, and photo for placement of shading and details.

Lining

Use #10/0 script liner brush.
❶ Using Dark Yellow-Green paint, line two short tendrils at base of pansy.
❷ Using Pale Green paint, line remaining four long tendrils. Some of these cross previously painted tendrils.

Base Coating

Use round brush and two coats.
❶ Using Pale Green paint, base-paint leaves.
❷ Using Light Purple paint, base-paint two back petals of pansy.
❸ Using Light Violet-Blue paint, base-paint two middle petals.
❹ Using Lilac paint, base-paint large front petal, including curled-over edges.

Shading

Use flat brush side loaded with paint. Refer to slash marks on pattern for placement.
❶ Using Dark Yellow-Green paint, shade leaves where they go behind pansy, along outer edges, and along midveins.
❷ Using Dark Purple paint, shade two back petals of pansy behind middle petals.
❸ Using Light Purple paint, shade areas behind front petal.
❹ Using Light Violet-Blue paint, shade under curled edges at top of front petal.
❺ Using Pure White paint, shade along left side of midvein and right edge of bottom leaf.

❻ Using Pure White paint, shade below midveins and along top edges of remaining leaves.
❼ Using Pure White paint, shade scalloped edges of pansy petals.

Details

Read Tips and Tricks on pg. 9 before beginning.
❶ Match traced outline of clock design with wood piece. Using stylus and white transfer paper, trace dots indicating clock positions and accent lines onto pansy petals.
❷ Using Butter Yellow paint, place a dot in center of pansy between curled edges. Pull dot upward into a teardrop shape, stopping where curved petals meet.
❸ Using Black paint, place a smaller dot in center of yellow paint dot. Pull it upward into a teardrop shape, stopping as before.
❹ Using Dark Purple paint, place accent lines on pansy petals.
❺ Using Pure White paint, place two dots side by side at top of Black teardrop. Pull each dot down and out (one to right and other to left) approximately ½", following top edge of front petal.
❻ Using Pale Pink paint, place a heart at end of each tendril.
❼ Using Pale Green paint, place five descending-sized dots at end of each heart.
❽ Using Medium Blue paint, place the dots which indicate clock positions.

Bow Hanger

Wooden bows come in many shapes, so shading will vary according to shape. Large Bow Detail pattern on pg. 103 illustrates proposed placement of detail lines (heavy lines indicate borders) and shading (slash marks). Use your own discretion when placing details and shading.
❶ Using flat brush side loaded with Medium Blue paint, shade bottom curve of all bow loops and ribbon tails where loops shadow them.
❷ Using #1 script liner brush and Pure White paint, line borders on loops, ribbons, and knot.

Finishing

Use adhesive/sealant to assemble.
❶ Use a damp cotton swab to remove remaining transfer lines.
❷ Using glaze brush, apply three coats of water-base varnish to all sides of clock and bow pieces. Let each coat dry separately.
❸ Attach eye hooks to bottom edge of bow and top edge of clock.
❹ Using pliers, attach ends of chain to eye hooks to join clock and bow.
❺ Attach an "O" hook to back of bow for hanging.
❻ Insert clockwork into clock and battery into clockwork.

Additional Ideas

❤ Hang chains from bottom of clock for a "cuckoo-clock" look.

❤ Hang wind chimes from bottom of clock, and hang in a patio or summer porch.

❤ Hang clock from a chain, and then place a fabric bow over the top of chain.

❤ Paint pansy buds or small hearts instead of dots for clock points.

❤ Paint a clock for each season, base painting each clock a different color. Or hang clock from a seasonal bow, as the seasons change.

❤ Instead of hanging from bow, hang from a sign that says, "Time Flies," "Time and Time Again," or "Spring Time." Or you can write the sayings on the clock itself.

❤ Use different wood cut-outs to hang clock, like a row of small hearts or flowers.

❤ Hang clock inside a pretty floral wreath or a frame painted to match.

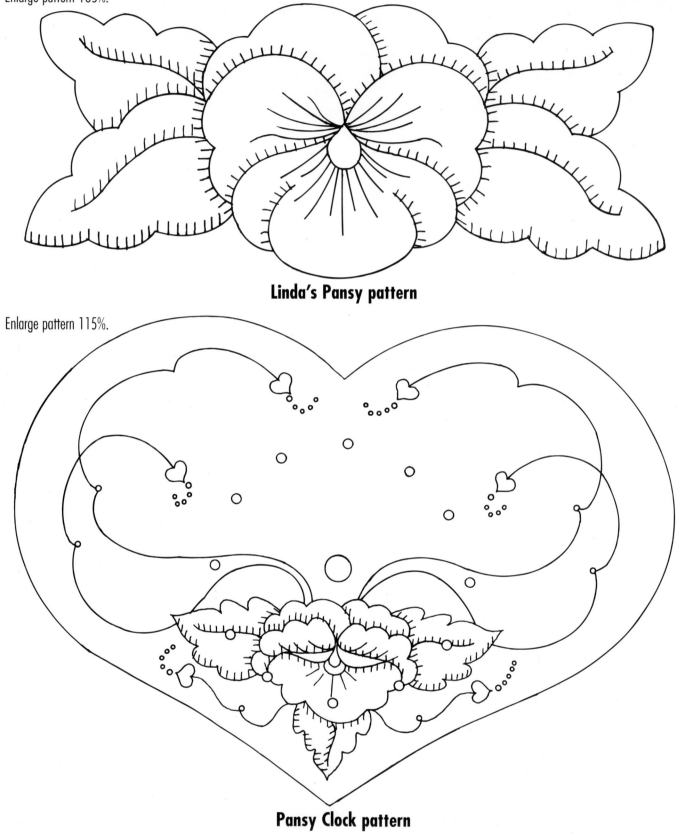

Enlarge pattern 105%.

Linda's Pansy pattern

Enlarge pattern 115%.

Pansy Clock pattern

Enlarge pattern 135%.

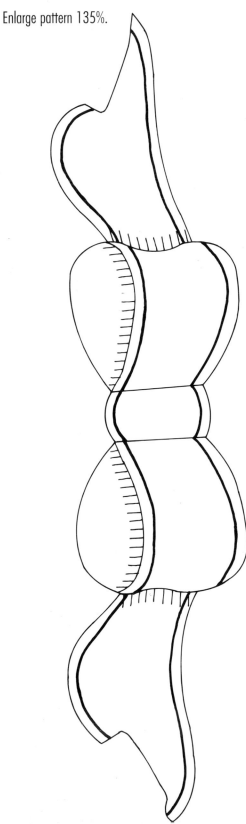

Pansy Clock Large Bow Detail pattern

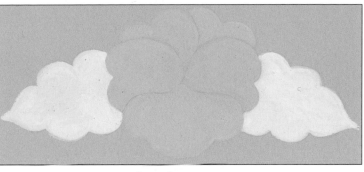

Base Coating

Shading

Accents

Highlighting
Linda's Pansy Colored Example

FRESH

f r e s h .
cherries

Designed by Lorna McRoden

Life is just a bowl of cherries! Read General Instructions before beginning any project. Trace Fresh Cherries patterns on pgs. 110 and 116 onto tracing paper, omitting slash marks which indicate shaded areas.

Specific Materials Needed

9" x 15" of ¾"-thick clear pine (clock and banner)
Clockwork
Two 2" lengths of ¼"-wide brass chain
Four brass eye hooks, ¼" dia.
One "0" ring hanger
Drill and ⁵⁄₁₆"-dia. bit
Scroll saw
All-purpose water-base sealer
Disposable sponge brush (1" wide)
White and colored transfer paper
Stylus
Flat brushes (#2 and #8)
Script liner brushes (#1 and #10/0)
Round brush (#2)
Glaze brush (¾" wide)
Water-base varnish
One AA battery
Needle-nose pliers
Adhesive/sealant

Acrylic Paint Palette

Medium Coral
Cadmium Red
Dark Wine Red
Very Pale Green
Dark Yellow-Green
Light Gray-Blue
Medium Blue
Medium Dark Blue
Dove Gray
Medium Yellow-Green
Soft White
Pure White

Preparation

❶ Using patterns and scroll saw, cut wood pieces.
❷ Center and glue top layer of central part of banner over bottom layer. Round edges of wood along folds in banner.
❸ With drill and bit, drill hole in center of clock piece as indicated on pattern.
❹ Prepare wood for painting, referring to Wood Preparation on pg. 8.
❺ Using disposable sponge brush, wash all sides of wood items with a mixture of ⅓ Soft White paint, ⅓ water, and ⅓ all-purpose water-base sealer. Usually two coats are needed. Let each coat dry separately. Lightly paper-sand after each coat.
❻ Match traced outline of clock design with wood piece. Using stylus and colored transfer paper, trace only bowl and leaves onto clock face. Trace banner designs on wood piece.

When painting dimensional items, paint one side and edges; let dry. Paint remaining side. Refer to pattern and photo for placement of shading and details.

Bowl

Using #2 flat brush and Medium Blue paint, base-paint band on bowl with two coats. Let each coat dry separately. Lightly paper-sand between each coat.

Leaves

Using round brush and Medium Yellow-Green paint, base-paint leaves with two coats.

Cherries

❶ Using #8 flat brush and Cadmium Red paint, base-paint cherry area with two coats.
❷ Match traced outline of clock design with wood piece. Using stylus and white transfer paper, trace outline and details of cherries only onto red-painted area.

Shading and Highlights

Use #2 flat brush side loaded with paint for steps 1—8. Refer to slash marks on pattern for placement of shading.
❶ Using Dove Gray paint, shade inside rim of bowl, under top lip, down sides, under bottom rim of bowl, around leaves, and along pleats in banner.
❷ Using Dark Wine Red paint, shade along bottom edges and behind curved edges of cherries. Shade inside stem indentations on cherries.
❸ Using Medium Coral paint, highlight around indentations and along top of cherries, following curved edges.
❹ Using Dark Yellow-Green paint, shade along midvein of each leaf. The single leaf should be shaded to left of midvein and others shaded to right of midvein.
❺ Using Dark Yellow-Green paint, shade single leaf along right scalloped edge and shade remaining leaves along left scalloped edges.
❻ Using Very Pale Green paint, highlight leaves along midveins, opposite dark shading, and along remaining unshaded edges.

❼ Using Very Pale Green paint, highlight underside of leaf tips.

❽ Using Medium Dark Blue paint, shade ends of band on bowl and shade band under leaves.

❾ Using #2 flat brush and Soft White paint, highlight blue band with three vertical lines.

Lining

Use #10/0 script liner brush for steps 2–5 and #1 script liner brush for steps 6–8.

❶ Match traced outline of clock design with wood piece. Using stylus and white transfer paper, trace stems, stem shadow line, and vein lines onto clock face.

❷ Using Medium Yellow-Green paint, paint stems. Let dry.

❸ Using Very Pale Green paint, highlight top edge of stem of cherry at right, and midveins and side veins on leaves.

❹ Using Light Gray-Blue paint, line inside top lip, under top lip, and along bottom rim of bowl.

❺ Using Pure White paint, outline top edge of cherries to separate.

❻ Using Pure White paint, place short fat lines at top of cherries for shine spots. Refer to pattern for placement.

❼ Using Dark Wine Red paint, line borders on banner and paint shadow line of stem of cherry at right.

❽ Using Medium Blue paint, line lettering on banner.

Dots and Heart Details

Read Tips and Tricks on pg. 9 before beginning.

❶ Using Medium Dark Blue paint, place dots on lettering on banner.

❷ Using Cadmium Red paint, place dots on border lines on banner.

❸ Using Cadmium Red paint, place hearts on banner and on bowl to indicate clock positions.

❹ Using Medium Yellow-Green paint, place dots between border lines on banner.

Finishing

Use adhesive/sealant to assemble.

❶ Use a damp cotton swab to remove remaining transfer lines.

❷ Using glaze brush, apply three coats of water-base varnish to all sides of clock pieces. Let each coat dry separately.

❸ Attach eye hooks to bottom edge of banner and top edge of clock.

❹ Using pliers, attach ends of chains to eye hooks to join clock and banner.

❺ Attach an "O" hook to back of banner for hanging.

❻ Insert clockwork into clock and battery into clockwork.

paper towels

Designed by Linda Alexander

Read General Instructions before beginning any project. Trace Paper Towel pattern on pg. 111 onto tracing paper, omitting slash marks and heavy lines which indicate shaded areas and accent lines.

Specific Materials Needed

7" x 12" of ¾"-thick clear pine (base and blossom/leaves)
Unfinished paper towel pin (1¼" dia. x 15" long)
⁵⁄₁₆"-dia. wood dowel (9")
*2 unfinished cherries/apples on a jute cord (2" dia.)
Drywall screw (1¼" long)
Brass eye hook (¼" dia.)
Drill and ⅛"- and ⁵⁄₁₆"-dia. bits
Scroll saw
All-purpose water-base sealer
Disposable sponge brush (1" wide)
Colored transfer paper
Stylus
Script liner brush (#10/0)
Flat brush (#6, #8, and #12)
Round brush (#2)
Clear matte spray acrylic finish
Adhesive/sealant

Acrylic Paint Palette

Light Pink
Bright Red
Pink
Butter Yellow
Pale Green
Medium Yellow-Green
Dark Yellow-Green
Medium Dark Teal
Medium Dark Blue
Medium Yellow-Brown
Soft White
Pure White

Preparation

❶ Using scroll saw, cut 6¾"-dia. circle from pine, and round edge on one side (top). Using pattern and scroll saw, cut out blossom/ leaves.

❷ Using drill and ⁵⁄₁₆"-dia. bit, drill a ½"-deep hole in top of base ¼" in from edge.

❸ Using drill and ⅛"-dia. bit, drill a hole in center bottom of base ¼" deep to countersink screw.

❹ Using drill and ¼"-dia. bit, drill a hole ¼ deep in bottom of blossom/leaves.

❺ Using drill and ⅛"-dia. bit, drill a ¼"-deep hole in top of cherries/apples.

❻ Prepare wood for painting, referring to Wood Preparation on pg. 8.

❼ Using disposable sponge brush, wash all sides of base, pin, and dowel stem with a mixture of ⅓ Medium Dark Blue paint, ⅓ water, and ⅓ all-purpose water-base sealer. Usually two coats are needed. Let each coat dry separately. Lightly paper-sand after each coat.

❽ Using #12 flat brush and a mixture of ⅓ Soft White paint, ⅓ water, and ⅓ all-purpose water-base sealer, wash all sides of cherry leaves using two coats. Let each coat dry separately. Lightly paper-sand after each coat.

❾ Using #12 flat brush and mixture of of ⅓ Bright Red paint, ⅓ water, and ⅓ all-purpose water-base sealer, wash all sides of wood cherries/apples using two coats. Let each coat dry separately. Lightly paper-sand after each coat.

❿ Match traced outline of cherry blossom and leaves pattern with wood piece. Using stylus and colored transfer paper, trace design.

When painting dimensional items, paint one side and edges; let dry. Paint remaining side. Refer to Colored Example on pg. 111, pattern, and photo for placement of shading and details.

Base Coating

Use round brush.

❶ Using Medium Yellow-Green paint, base-paint leaf on left side of blossom.

❷ Using Pale Green paint, base-paint leaf on right side of blossom.

❸ Using Light Pink paint, base-paint five blossom petals.

❹ Using Butter Yellow paint, base-paint blossom center.

Shading

Refer to slash marks on pattern for placement.

❶ Using #8 flat brush side loaded with Medium Dark Teal paint, shade left leaf along bottom edge, above midvein, and where it goes behind blossom.

❷ Using #8 flat brush side loaded with Dark Yellow-Green paint, shade right leaf along bottom edge, above midvein, and where it goes behind blossom.

❸ Using #6 flat brush side loaded with Pink paint, shade base of each blossom petal.

❹ Using #6 flat brush side loaded with Medium Yellow-Brown paint, shade bottom edge of blossom center.

Highlighting

❶ Using #8 flat brush side loaded with Pale Green paint, highlight left leaf along top edge and below midvein.

❷ Using #8 flat brush side loaded with Pure White paint, highlight right leaf along top edge and below midvein.

❸ Using #6 flat brush side loaded with Pure White paint, highlight outer edges of five blossom petals.

Details

Refer to Tips and Tricks on pg. 9 before beginning.

❶ Using script liner brush and Pure White paint, line mid and side veins of leaves.

❷ Using stylus and Dark Yellow-Green paint, randomly place tiny dots on blossom petals near center. Refer to photo and Colored Example on pg. 111 for placement.

Finishing

Use adhesive/sealant to assemble.

❶ Use a damp cotton swab to remove remaining transfer lines.

❷ Spray all sides of wood items with matte spray acrylic finish. Apply three coats, letting each coat dry thoroughly.

❸ Use screw and glue to secure blunt end of towel pin to center of base.

❹ Apply a small amount of glue to one end of remaining dowel. Insert into remaining hole in base.

❺ Screw eye hook into bottom of blossom/leaves just in front of hole (cherry will hang below design, so hook should be placed on that side of hole).

❻ Fold jute cord in half and push cord through eye hook. Tie an overhand knot ¾" from fold.

❼ Apply a small amount of glue to fold of cord. Push cord into hole in blossom/leaves unit.

❽ Apply a small amount of glue to remaining end of dowel. Slide design piece onto dowel. Design should face outward.

If a cherry/apple unit is not available, buy two 2"-dia. unfinished cherries/apples and cut a 5" length of ⅛"-dia. jute cord. Using ⅛"-dia. drill bit, drill holes in cherry tops. Paint and let dry. Place glue in holes and push an end of jute cord into each one. Let dry and continue with step 6 of Finishing.

Additional Ideas

♥ Hang different fruits from towel holder to suit the season. Some fruits you could hang are strawberries, apples, oranges, lemons, grapes, or peaches. You can paint the towel holder to match fruit if desired.

♥ Use a poinsettia for the blossom/leaves, and hang jingle bells, miniature ornaments, or mistletoe from the poinsettia.

♥ Paint oak leaves and hang an acorn from leaves. Or paint lettuce leaves and hang miniature veggies from them.

bluebirds &
cherries

Designed by Lorna McRoden

Read General Instructions before beginning any project. Trace Bluebirds & Cherries patterns on opposite page onto tracing paper.

Specific Materials Needed

Unfinished-wood double switch plate
Unfinished-wood bird (2" wide x 4" long)
All-purpose water-base sealer
Stylus
Colored transfer paper
2 artificial rose leaves with stems (¾" long)
Two 10mm wood balls (cherries)
¼"-dia. wood dowel (4")
Disposable sponge brushes (1" wide)
Script liner brush (#10/0)
Round brush (#3)
Toothpick
Drill and ¹⁄₁₆"-dia. bit
Clear matte spray acrylic finish
Adhesive/sealant

Acrylic Paint Palette

Bright Red
Golden Yellow
Medium Yellow-Green
Dark Yellow-Green
Medium Blue
Medium Dark Blue
Medium Yellow-Brown
Black
Soft White

Preparation

❶ Prepare wood for painting, referring to Wood Preparation on pg. 8.
❷ Using a disposable sponge brush, wash all sides of switch plate with a mixture of ⅓ Soft White paint, ⅓ water, and ⅓ all-purpose water-base sealer. Usually two coats are needed. Let each coat dry separately. Lightly paper-sand after each coat.
❸ Using a disposable sponge brush, wash all sides of bird with a mixture of ⅓ Medium Blue paint, ⅓ water, and ⅓ all-purpose water-base sealer. Usually two coats are needed. Let each coat dry separately. Lightly paper-sand after each coat.
❹ Match traced outline of Bluebird motif with wood piece. Using stylus and transfer paper, trace beak and eye. Turn tracing paper over so that design is reversed and retrace beak and eye onto other side of wood.
❺ Match outline of switch plate design with wood piece. Using stylus and transfer paper, trace Switch Plate motif.

Refer to Colored Example on opposite page, pattern, and photo for placement of details.

Base Coating

Use two coats.

❶ Using round brush and Medium Dark Blue paint, paint recessed edge of switch plate.
❷ Using round brush and Bright Red paint, paint wood balls.

Lining and Details

Refer to Tips and Tricks on pg. 9, and to pattern and photo for placement.

❶ Using script liner brush and Dark Yellow-Green paint, line cherry stems on switch plate.
❷ Using script liner brush and Medium Blue paint, line quilt lines on switch plate.
❸ Using round brush and Golden Yellow paint, paint bird's beak, carrying color onto edges. Using script liner brush and Medium Yellow-Brown paint, line smile line on bird's beak.
❹ Using back end of script liner brush and Soft White paint, place a dot for bird's eye. Let dry.
❺ Using stylus and Black paint, place a smaller dot in center of eye. Let dry.
❻ Using toothpick and Soft White paint, place a smaller dot in center of Black dot in eye. Let dry.
❼ Using end of wood dowel and Bright Red paint, place a dot for each cherry. Let dry.
❽ Using handle end of script liner brush and Medium Yellow-Green paint, place dots near top of each cherry stem (one on each side of stem). While paint is still wet, use stylus to pull dots up into teardrop shapes to make leaves.
❾ Using stylus and Dark Yellow-Green paint, place a dot between each leaf pair.
❿ Using stylus and Soft White paint, place a highlight dot on each cherry.

Repeat steps 3–6 for other side of bird.

Finishing

Use adhesive/sealant to assemble.

❶ Use a damp cotton swab to remove remaining transfer lines.
❷ Spray all sides of wood items using matte spray acrylic finish. Apply three coats, letting each coat dry separately.
❸ Using drill and bit, drill a hole through bird's beak from top to bottom and ¼" from tip.

❹ Using drill and bit, drill a hole halfway through each ball.
❺ Glue wings to bird. Refer to pattern for placement.
❻ Twist rose leaves stems together, and thread through hole in beak, and then separate stems.
❼ Thread a ball onto each stem, and glue in place.
❽ Glue bird to center top front of switch plate.

Enlarge pattern 120%.

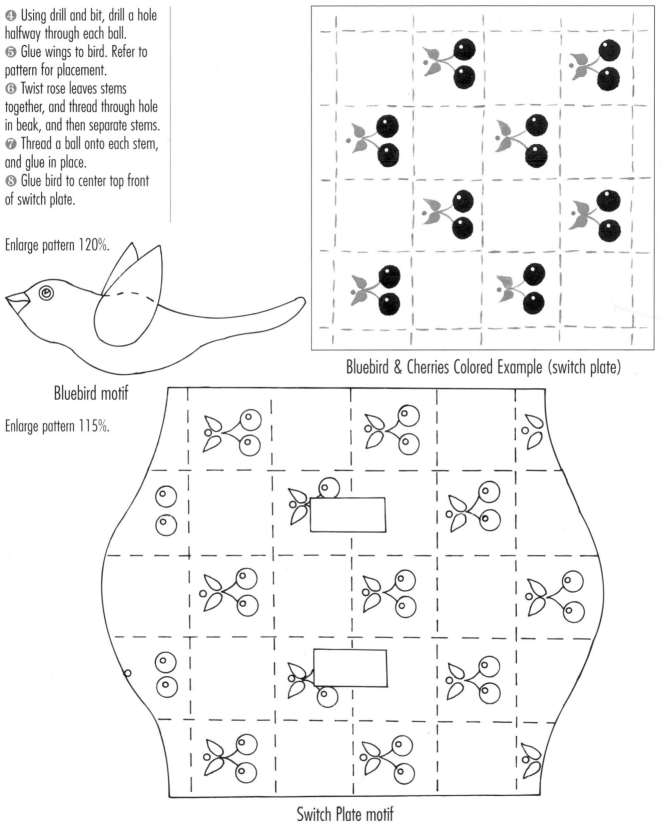

Bluebird motif

Enlarge pattern 115%.

Bluebird & Cherries Colored Example (switch plate)

Switch Plate motif
Bluebird & Cherries patterns

Enlarge patterns 120%.

Fresh Cherries patterns

Pattern full size.

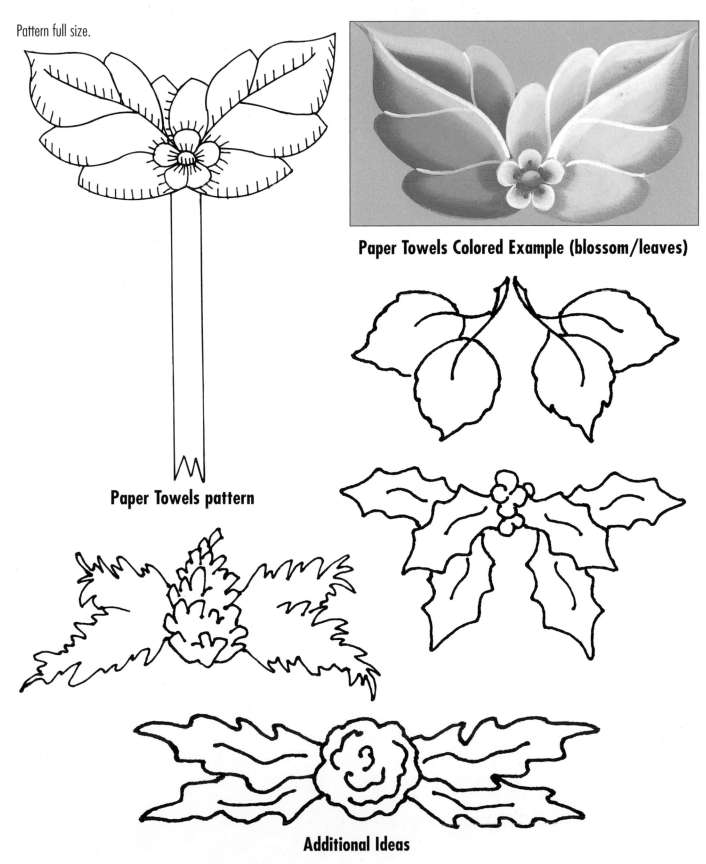

Paper Towels Colored Example (blossom/leaves)

Paper Towels pattern

Additional Ideas

a p p l e
t i m e

Designed by Lorna McRoden

Near our homes is an area called "Apple Hill." Every fall people come from all over the country to buy fresh apples, apple cider, and pies when it's apple time.

Read General Instructions before beginning any project. Trace Apple Time patterns on pgs. 116 and 117 onto tracing paper, omitting slash marks which indicate shaded areas.

Specific Materials Needed

9" x 15" of ¾"-thick clear pine (clock and banner)
Clockwork
Two 2" lengths of ¼"-wide brass chain
Four brass eye hooks (¼" dia.)
One "O" ring hanger
Drill and 5⁄16"-dia. bit
Scroll saw
All-purpose water-base sealer
Disposable sponge brush (1" wide)
Stylus
Round brushes (#2 and #4)
White and colored transfer paper
Script liner brushes (#1 and #10/0)
Flat brush (#8)

Glaze brush (¾" wide)
Water-base varnish
One AA battery
Needle-nose pliers
Adhesive/sealant

Acrylic Paint Palette

Medium Coral
Cadmium Red
Dark Red
Very Dark Red
Very Pale Green
Pale Green
Dark Yellow-Green
Medium Brown
Medium Dark Teal
Light Gray-Blue
Medium Blue
Pale Blue
Soft White

Preparation

❶ Using patterns and scroll saw, cut wood pieces.
❷ Using adhesive/sealant, center and glue top layer of central part of banner over bottom layer. Round edges of wood along folds in banner.

❸ Using drill and bit, drill hole in center of clock piece, as indicated on pattern.
❹ Prepare wood for painting, referring to Wood Preparation on pg. 8.
❺ Using disposable sponge brush, wash all sides of wood items with a mixture of ⅓ Soft White paint, ⅓ water, and ⅓ all-purpose water-base sealer. Usually two coats are needed. Let each coat dry separately. Lightly paper-sand after each coat.
❻ Match traced outline of clock design with wood piece. Using stylus and colored transfer paper, trace only bowl and leaves onto clock face. Trace banner designs onto wood piece.

When painting dimensional items, paint one side and edges; let dry. Paint remaining side. Refer to pattern and photo for placement of shading and details.

Bowl

Using flat brush side loaded with Pale Blue paint, shade under top lip of bowl, around leaves, under bottom rim of bowl, and along pleats in banner.

Apples

Use #4 round brush for steps 1, 3, and 4. Use flat brush side loaded with paint for steps 5–9. Refer to slash marks on pattern for placement of shading. Let dry between steps.
❶ Using Cadmium Red paint, base-paint apple area with two coats of paint.
❷ Match traced outline of clock design with wood piece. Using stylus and white transfer paper, trace outlines and dashed lines in apples onto apple area.
❸ Using Dark Red paint, paint lower halves of apples below broken lines and core indentations.
❹ Using Medium Coral paint, highlight area above dotted line on front apple.
❺ Using Dark Red paint, blend hard edge of Dark Red paint into Cadmium Red painted areas, creating a soft transition between paint colors on apples.
❻ Using Medium Coral paint, blend hard edge of Medium Coral paint into Cadmium Red painted area on front apple.
❼ Using Medium Brown paint, shade inside areas of indentations and lowest portions of apples.
❽ Using Medium Coral paint, shade apples around outer areas of indentations.
❾ Using Soft White paint, shade apples around outer areas of indentations and along top edge of front apple, blending paint into Medium Coral area.

Refer to photo for placement. Using #2 round brush and Dark Red paint, paint accent lines on apples. Place these lines perpendicular to blended lines, leaving space between each line so that base color will still show. Start in Dark Red areas pulling color up into Cadmium Red areas.

Stems, Apples, and Leaves

Use flat brush side loaded with paint for steps 2 and 4–8. Use #2 round brush for step 3. Refer to slash marks on pattern for placement of shading.

❶ Match traced outline of clock design with wood piece. Using stylus and white transfer paper, trace stem and its shadow onto apple, stem onto bowl, dew drops onto apples, and detail lines in indentations of apples.

❷ Using Soft White paint, paint dew drops on apples.

❸ Using Pale Green paint, basepaint leaves with two coats.

❹ Using Dark Yellow-Green paint, shade underside of lower leaf's curled tip.

❺ Using Medium Dark Teal paint, shade lower leaf along right side of midvein and shadow along left scalloped edge.

❻ Using Medium Dark Teal paint, shade upper leaf adjacent to front apple, along right-hand side of midvein, along left scalloped edge, and along scalloped edge at tip.

❼ Using Very Pale Green paint, highlight lower leaf along left side of midvein, right scalloped edge, and tip of leaf.

❽ Using Very Pale Green paint, highlight upper leaf along left side of midvein and right scalloped edge.

Lining and Highlighting

Use #1 script liner brush for steps 1, 5, 7, and 8 and #10/0 script liner brush for steps 2, 3, 4, and 6. Refer to pattern for placement of dew drop details in steps 3 and 5.

❶ Using Medium Brown paint, paint stems of apples. Let dry.

❷ Using Pale Green paint, highlight accent lines in indentations of apples, highlight one edge of each stem, and fill in stem ends.

❸ Using Soft White paint, highlight leaves along their midveins and side veins, place highlight dots on dew drops, paint an accent line along left edge of each dew drop, and highlight lines dividing apples.

❹ Using Very Dark Red paint, paint stem shadow of apple at left, and line along bottoms and right edges of dew drops to create a shadow.

❺ Using Pale Blue paint, paint stem shadow of front apple.

❻ Using Light Gray-Blue paint, line inside top lip, under top lip, and along bottom rim of bowl.

❼ Using Medium Blue paint, line two bands around middle of bowl and borders on banner.

❽ Using Medium Dark Teal paint, line lettering on banner.

Dots and Heart Details

Read Tips and Tricks and Layering on pg. 9 before painting details.

❶ Using Pale Green paint, place dots on lettering on banner.

❷ Using Soft White paint, place a heart on stem of front apple.

❸ Using Cadmium Red paint, place hearts on banner and on bowl to indicate clock positions.

Finishing

Use adhesive/sealant to assemble.

❶ Use a damp cotton swab to remove remaining transfer lines.

❷ Using glaze brush, apply three coats of water-base varnish to all sides of clock pieces. Let each coat dry separately.

❸ Attach eye hooks to bottom edge of banner and top edge of clock.

❹ Using pliers, attach ends of chain to eye hooks to join clock and banner.

❺ Attach an "O" hook to back of banner for hanging.

❻ Insert clockwork into clock and battery into clockwork.

Additional Ideas

❤ Instead of making a clock, make a door hanger and write your family name on the banner.

❤ Paint peaches instead of apples and write "Just Peachy" on the banner.

❤ Paint lemons instead of apples and write "Make Lemonade!" on the banner.

❤ Paint oranges instead of apples and write "Juicy!" on the banner.

❤ Write "An Apple a Day" on the banner.

❤ Paint a cute worm with a ruler and a graduate's cap on the banner and give it to your favorite teacher.

❤ Use a wooden heart instead of an apple for the William Tell bookends. Display on Valentine's Day.

❤ Paint William Tell bookends in pinks and reds. Instead of apple slices attach a small wooden cupid with bow and arrows to each bookend.

william tell

Designed by Linda Alexander

Read General Instructions before beginning any project. Tracc William Tell patterns on pg. 116 onto tracing paper, omitting slash marks which indicate shaded areas.

Specific Materials Needed

10" sq. of ½"-thick clear plywood
Unfinished-wood heart (1½" wide x ½" thick)
Unfinished-wood apple (2½" dia.)
¼"-dia. dowel (5¼")
Two finishing nails (1" long)
Drill and ¼"-dia. bit
Band saw
Wood filler
All-purpose water-base sealer
Disposable sponge brushes (1" wide)
White and colored transfer paper
Stylus
Flat brush (#8)
Script liner brush (#10/0)
Round brush (#1)
Glaze brush (¾" wide)
Water-base varnish
Adhesive/sealant

Acrylic Paint Palette

Napthol Crimson
Pale Green
Medium Yellow-Green
Dark Yellow-Green
Medium Dark Blue
Soft White
Pure White

Preparation

❶ Using patterns and band saw, cut two backs, two bases, and one fletch (the feather like end of an arrow).

❷ Cut wood apple in half vertically. Sand.

❸ Using drill and bit, drill a hole through fletch coming out at point, a ½"-deep hole in top of heart coming out at point, and a ½"-deep hole in each side of apple 1½" up from bottom, aligning holes horizontally.

❹ Prepare wood for painting, referring to Wood Preparation on pg. 8.

❺ Using disposable sponge brush, wash all sides of bookends with a mixture of ⅓ Medium Dark Blue paint, ⅓ water, and ⅓ all-purpose water-base sealer.

Usually two coats are needed. Let each coat dry separately. Lightly paper-sand after each coat.

❻ Using disposable sponge brush, wash fletch with a mixture of ⅓ Soft White paint, ⅓ water, and ⅓ all-purpose water-base sealer. Usually two coats are needed. Let each coat dry separately. Lightly paper-sand after each coat.

❼ Using disposable sponge brush, wash all sides of heart arrowhead and apple halves with a mixture of ⅓ Napthol Crimson paint, ⅓ water, and ⅓ all-purpose water-base sealer.

❽ Match traced outline of bookend design with a wood piece. Using stylus and white transfer paper, trace design. Repeat for other bookend.

❾ Match traced outline of fletch design with its wood piece. Using stylus and colored transfer paper, trace design.

When painting dimensional items, paint one side and edges; let dry. Paint remaining sides. Refer to patterns and photo for placement of details and shading.

Fletch

Using flat brush and Medium Dark Blue paint, base-paint chevron on both sides of fletch, carrying color across top and bottom edges to join.

Leaves

Refer to slash marks on pattern for placement of shading.

❶ Using script liner brush and Pale Green paint, line tendrils behind leaves on bookends.

❷ Using round brush and Medium Yellow-Green paint, base-paint leaf on left using two coats.

❸ Using round brush and Pale Green paint, base-paint leaf on right using two coats.

❹ Using script liner brush and Medium Yellow-Green paint, line two leaf stems.

❺ Using flat brush side loaded with Dark Yellow-Green paint, shade left leaf along left side of midvein and along edge where it joins right leaf.

❻ Using flat brush side loaded with Dark Yellow-Green paint, shade right leaf along left side of midvein and along scalloped right edge.

❼ Using flat brush side loaded with Pure White paint, highlight along each midvein and along scalloped left edges of each leaf.

Details

Refer to Tips and Tricks on pg. 9 before beginning.

❶ Using handle end of a brush and Napthol Crimson paint, place a heart at end of each tendril and place one between leaves at top of designs.

❷ Using handle end of a brush and Pale Green paint, place three descending-sized dots below each heart and place a dot on corner of each tendril.

Finishing

Use adhesive/sealant to assemble.

❶ Use a damp cotton swab to remove remaining transfer lines.

❷ Using glaze brush, apply three coats of water-base varnish to all sides of pieces. Let each coat dry separately.

❸ Assemble and glue base and back pieces together, forming an "L." Secure with finishing nails.

❹ Countersink nails. Fill holes with wood filler.

❺ Center cut edge of each apple within design area on a back piece of each bookend. Glue in place. Let dry.

❻ Cut dowel to a 2¾" length. Apply glue to one end. Insert into one hole in apple.

❼ Apply glue to other end. Slide fletch onto end.

❽ Apply glue to one end of remaining dowel. Insert into hole in other apple.

❾ Apply glue to other end. Slide heart onto end.

Enlarge Fletch pattern 110%.
Enlarge Back and Base patterns 125%.

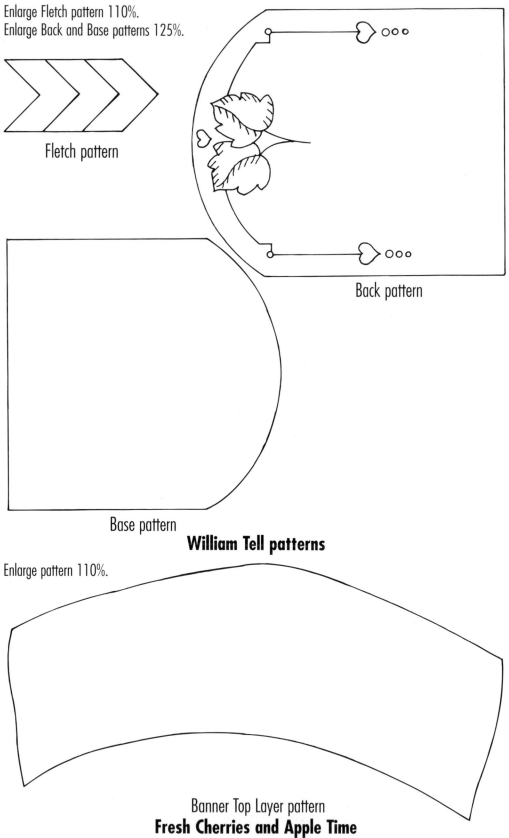

Fletch pattern

Back pattern

Base pattern

William Tell patterns

Enlarge pattern 110%.

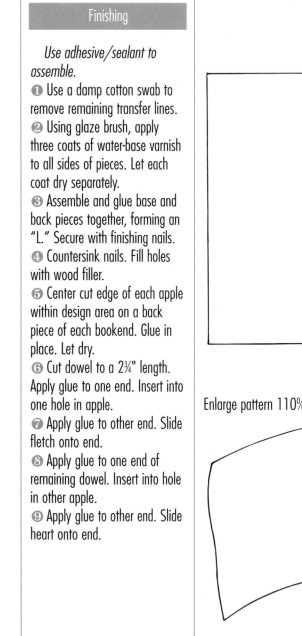

Banner Top Layer pattern
Fresh Cherries and Apple Time

Enlarge patterns 115%.

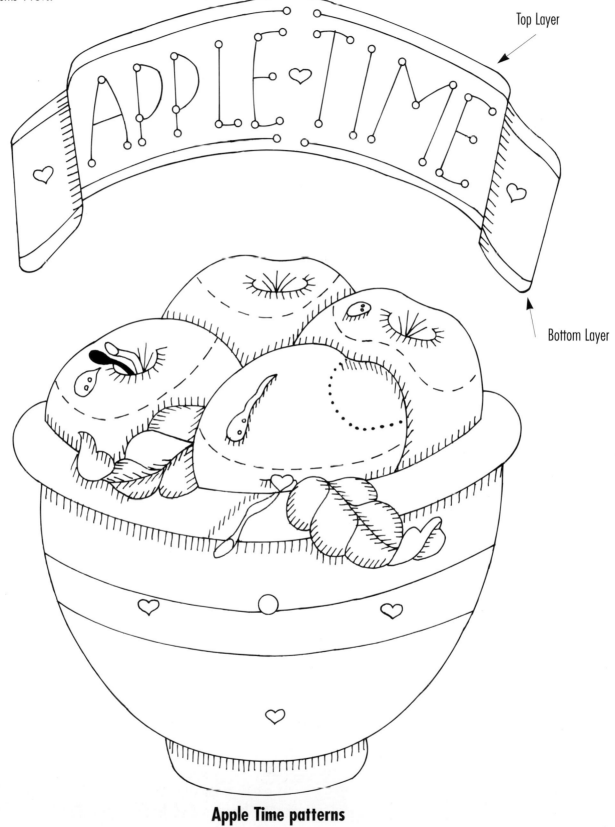

Top Layer

Bottom Layer

Apple Time patterns

o a k   l e a v e s   &

a c o r n s

Designed by John and Linda Alexander

This dimensional design can be adapted to fit most unfinished corner shelves.

Read General Instructions before beginning any project. Trace Oak Leaves & Acorns patterns on pg. 120 onto tracing paper, omitting slash marks which indicate shaded areas.

Unfinished corner shelf (12" tall)
12" sq. of ⅛"-thick birch plywood (leaves)
Colored and white transfer paper
Stylus
Scroll saw
Stain controller/wood sealer
Oak-colored stain
All-purpose water-base sealer
Wooden acorn (1½" high)
Disposable sponge brushes (1" wide)
Flat brushes (#8 and #12)
Script liner brush (#10/0)
Clear matte spray acrylic finish
Adhesive/sealant
Two "O" ring hangers (optional)

Acrylic Paint Palette

Pale Green
Light Yellow-Green
Medium Yellow-Brown
Medium Dark Teal
Teal Green

Preparation

❶ Using stylus and colored transfer paper, trace six leaf outlines onto plywood. Cut out using scroll saw.
❷ Prepare wood for painting and staining, referring to Wood Preparation on pg. 8.
❸ Using a disposable sponge brush, seal and stain all sides of corner shelf and acorn. Let dry. Lightly paper-sand.
❹ Using a disposable sponge brush and Teal Green paint, paint front edges of shelves. Usually two coats are needed. Let each coat dry separately. Lightly paper-sand after each coat.
❺ Using #8 flat brush and Medium Yellow-Brown paint, paint acorn cap. Usually two coats are needed. Let each coat dry separately. Lightly paper-sand after each coat.

❻ Using #12 flat brush, wash all sides of leaves with a mixture of ⅓ Medium Dark Teal paint, ⅓ water, and ⅓ all-purpose water-base sealer. Usually two coats are needed. Lightly paper-sand after each coat.
❼ Match traced outline of each leaf design with a wood piece. Using stylus and white transfer paper, trace midveins and side veins.

When painting dimensional items, paint one side and edges; let dry. Paint remaining side. Refer to Colored Example on pg. 120, patterns, and photo for placement of shading and details.

Shading and Highlighting

Use #8 flat brush side loaded with paint. Refer to slash marks on patterns for placement of shading.
❶ Using Teal Green paint, shade leaves along bottom edges and above midveins.
❷ Using Light Yellow-Green paint, highlight leaves along top edges and below midveins.

Details

Using script liner brush and Pale Green paint, line midveins and side veins of each leaf.

Finishing

❶ Use a damp cotton swab to remove remaining transfer lines.
❷ Spray all sides of wood items with matte spray acrylic finish. Apply three coats, letting each coat dry separately.
❸ Using adhesive/sealant, center and glue leaves to top shelf edge. Refer to photo for placement. Leaves are arranged in descending sizes (from center out to right and to left). Glue acorn to center of leaves.
❹ Attach "O" ring hangers, if desired, following manufacturer's directions.

Additional Ideas

❤ Instead of an acorn, paint a wooden flower to go in the center of the leaves.

❤ Paint holly leaves and glue berries or bells to the center for Christmas. Or, make snowflake "leaves" and glue a star in the center.

❤ Use miniature ballet slippers and a ballerina, or baseball bats, balls, and mitts for children's rooms.

Enlarge patterns 105%.

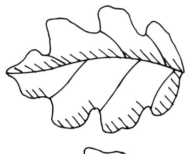

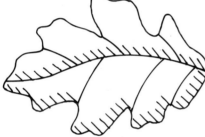

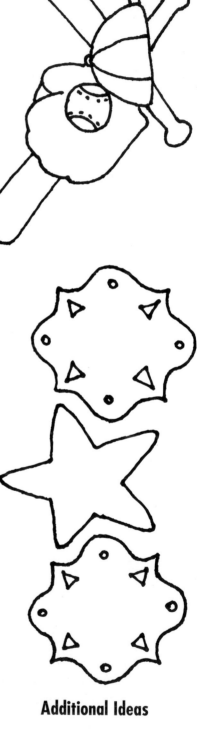

Oak Leaves & Acorns patterns

Oak Leaves & Acorns Colored Example

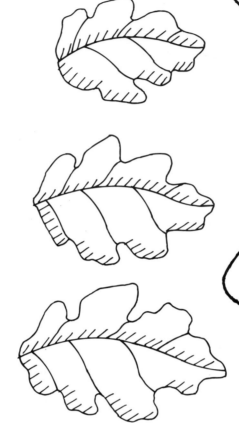

Additional Ideas

bow-tied quilts

Designed by Lorna McRoden

Read General Instructions before beginning any project. Trace Bow-Tied Quilt Backboard pattern on pg. 125 onto tracing paper.

Specific Materials Needed

Unfinished three-dimensional bow (2¾" wide x 12" long)
6" x 11" of ¾"-thick clear pine (backboard)
Two 1"-dia. wood dowels (6½")
Two ½"-dia. wood dowels (1½")
Drill and ⅛"-, ¼"-, and ½"-dia. bits
Scroll saw
All-purpose water-base sealer
Disposable sponge brush (1" wide)
Script liner brush (#1)
Flat brush (#12)
Glaze brush (¾" wide)
Water-base varnish
Adhesive/sealant

Acrylic Paint Palette

Light Pink
Pink
Pure White

Preparation

❶ Using pattern and scroll saw, cut out backboard. Round edges on one side of backboard.
❷ Using drill and ½"-dia. bit, drill two holes in backboard. Refer to pattern for placement.
❸ Using drill and ½"-dia. bit, drill out centers of 1"-dia. dowels.
❹ Apply adhesive/sealant to one end of each of dowel tubes. Insert into holes in backboard. Let dry.
❺ Using drill and ¼"-dia. bit, drill two holes in backboard 1" to right and to left of dowel tubes.
❻ Center back of bow over dowels in backboard. Mark bow.
❼ Using drill and ½"-dia. bit, drill two ¼"-deep holes in center of marks. The placement must be accurate, as these dowels will slide into dowel tubes.
❽ Apply adhesive/sealant to one end of each of ½"-dia. dowels, and insert into holes in back of bow. Let dry.
❾ Prepare wood for painting, referring to Wood Preparation on pg. 8.
❿ Using disposable sponge brush, wash all sides of bow and

backboard (leave dowels unfinished) with a mixture of ⅓ Light Pink paint, ⅓ water, and ⅓ all-purpose water-base sealer. Usually two coats are needed. Let each coat dry separately. Lightly paper-sand after each coat.

When painting dimensional items, paint one side and edges; let dry. Paint remaining side. Refer to slash marks and heavy lines on Large Bow Detail pattern for placement of shading and detail lines.

Wooden bows come in many shapes, so shading will vary according to shape. Large Bow Detail pattern illustrates proposed placement of detail lines (heavy lines indicate borders) and shading (slash marks). Use your own discretion when placing details and shading.

Shading

Using flat brush side loaded with Pink paint, shade bow loops and ribbon tails where loops shadow.

Lining

Using script liner brush and Pure White paint, line borders on loops, ribbons, and knot.

Finishing

Use adhesive/sealant to assemble.
❶ Using glaze brush, apply three coats of water-base varnish to all sides of wood pieces. Let each coat dry separately.
❷ Slide bow into backboard.

Additional Ideas

❤ Try using the shapes and paint patterns below and on the following pages.

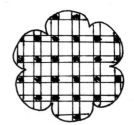

bow-tied
towels

Designed by Lorna McRoden

Read General Instructions before beginning any project. Trace Bow-Tied Towels Backboard pattern on pg. 125 onto tracing paper.

Specific Materials Needed

Unfinished three-dimensional bow (1½" wide x 6" long)
4" sq. of ½"-thick clear pine (backboard)
Two ⅜"-dia. wood dowels (2¾")
Drill and ⅜"-dia. bits
Scroll saw
"O" ring hanger
All-purpose water-base sealer
Disposable sponge brush (1" wide)
Script liner brush (#10/0)
Flat brush (#12)
Glaze brush (¾" wide)
Water-base varnish
Adhesive/sealant

Acrylic Paint Palette

Light Yellow-Green
Dark Yellow-Green
Soft White
Pure White

Preparation

❶ Using pattern and scroll saw, cut out backboard.

❷ Using drill and ⅜"-dia. bit, drill two holes in backboard. Refer to pattern for placement.

❸ Apply adhesive/sealant to one end of each dowel. Insert dowels into holes in backboard. Let dry.

❹ Center back of bow over dowels in backboard. Mark bow.

❺ Using drill and ⅜"-dia. bit, drill two holes on marks in back of bow, ¼" deep. The placement must be accurate, as dowels will slide into holes.

❻ Apply adhesive/sealant to remaining end of each dowel. Insert into holes in back of bow. Let dry.

❼ Prepare wood pieces for painting, referring to Wood Preparation on pg. 8.

❽ Using disposable sponge brush, wash all sides of bow (leave dowels unfinished) with a mixture of ⅓ Light Yellow-Green paint, ⅓ water, and ⅓ all-purpose water-base sealer. Usually two coats are needed. Let each coat dry separately. Lightly paper-sand after each coat.

❾ Using disposable sponge brush, wash all sides of heart backing piece with a mixture of ⅓ Soft White paint, ⅓ water, and ⅓ all-purpose water-base sealer. Usually two coats are needed. Let each coat dry separately. Lightly paper-sand after each coat.

When painting dimensional items, paint one side and edges; let dry. Paint remaining side. Refer to slash marks and heavy lines on Medium Bow Detail pattern for placement of shading and detail lines.

Wooden bows come in many shapes, so shading will vary according to shape. Medium Bow Detail pattern illustrates proposed placement of detail lines (heavy lines indicate borders) and shading (slash marks). Use your own discretion when placing details and shading.

Shading

Using flat brush side loaded with Dark Yellow-Green paint, shade bow loops and ribbon tails where loops shadow.

Lining

Using script liner brush and Pure White paint, line borders on loops, ribbons, and knot.

Finishing

Use adhesive/sealant to assemble.

❶ Using glaze brush, apply three coats of water-base varnish to all sides of pieces. Let each coat dry separately.

❷ Attach "O" ring to back of backboard for hanging.

Additional Ideas

bow-tied coat hook

Designed by Lorna McRoden

Read General Instructions before beginning any project. Slash marks on pattern indicate shaded areas.

Specific Materials Needed

Unfinished three-dimensional bow (1⅞" wide x 9¼" long)
Brass ceiling hook, size #8 (6" long)
1"-dia. wood knob
Drill and ¼"-dia. bit
Two "O" ring hangers
All-purpose water-base sealer
Stylus
Disposable sponge brush (1" wide)
Script liner brush (#1)
Flat brush (#12)
Clear matte spray acrylic finish
Adhesive/sealant
Soft lead pencil

Acrylic Paint Palette

Medium Pink
Light Yellow-Green
Pale Teal
Medium Dark Teal
Pure White

Preparation

❶ Prepare wood for painting, referring to Wood Preparation on pg. 8.
❷ Using drill and bit, drill a ¼"-deep hole in knob and on bottom edge of bow at its center.
❸ Using disposable sponge brush, wash all sides of bow with a mixture of ⅓ Pale Teal paint, ⅓ water, and ⅓ all-purpose water-base sealer. Usually two coats are needed. Let each coat dry separately. Lightly paper-sand after each coat.
❹ Using flat brush, wash all sides of knob with a mixture of ⅓ Medium Dark Teal paint, ⅓ water, and ⅓ all-purpose water-base sealer. Usually two coats are needed. Let each coat dry separately. Lightly paper-sand after each coat.
❺ Using soft lead pencil, sketch design on Bow-Tied Coat Hook pattern on pg. 126 onto bow.

When painting dimensional items, paint one side and edges and let dry. Then paint remaining side. Refer to pattern and photo for placement of shading, lining, and details.

Shading

Refer to slash marks on pattern for placement.

Using flat brush side loaded with Medium Dark Teal paint, shade bow loops and ribbon tails where loops shadow.

Lining

❶ Using script liner brush and Pure White paint, line bow loops, knot, and ribbon tails. Refer to heavy lines on pattern for placement.
❷ Using script liner brush, Light Yellow-Green, and Pure White paint, line remaining horizontal and vertical "plaid" lines on bow.

Details

Refer to Tips and Tricks on pg. 9 before beginning.

❶ Using handle end of script liner brush and Medium Pink paint, make hearts on bow.
❷ Using stylus and Light Yellow-Green paint, make two small dots above and below heart on knot.

Finishing

Use adhesive/sealant for assembly.

❶ Spray all sides of wood with matte spray acrylic finish. Apply three coats, letting each coat dry separately.
❷ Apply adhesive/sealant to threaded end of hook. Insert it into hole in bow.
❸ Apply adhesive/sealant to other end of hook. Insert it into hole in knob.
❹ Attach "O" ring hangers to back of bow.

Additional Ideas

Enlarge pattern 160%.

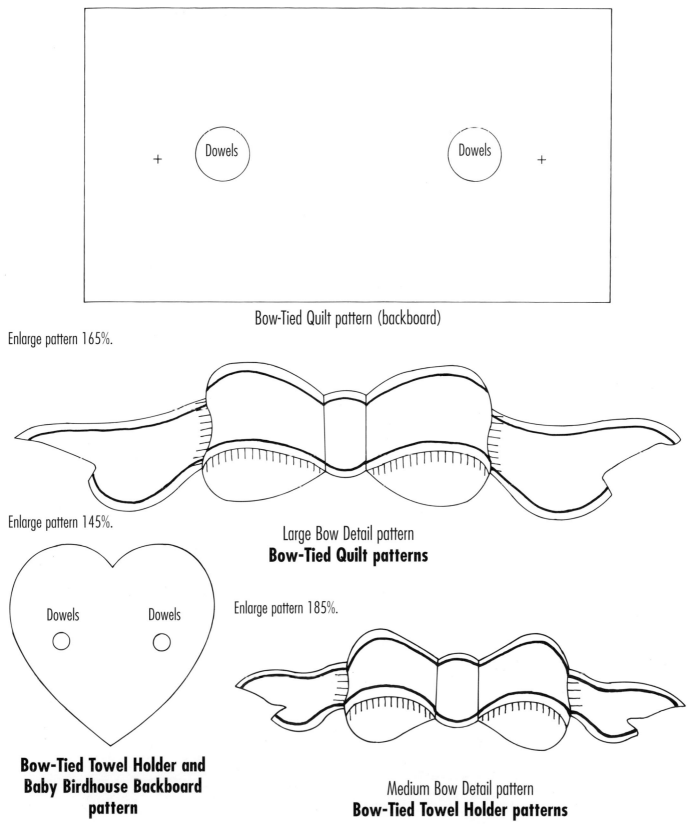

Bow-Tied Quilt pattern (backboard)

Enlarge pattern 165%.

Large Bow Detail pattern
Bow-Tied Quilt patterns

Enlarge pattern 145%.

Dowels   Dowels

**Bow-Tied Towel Holder and
Baby Birdhouse Backboard
pattern**

Enlarge pattern 185%.

Medium Bow Detail pattern
Bow-Tied Towel Holder patterns

Enlarge pattern 130%.

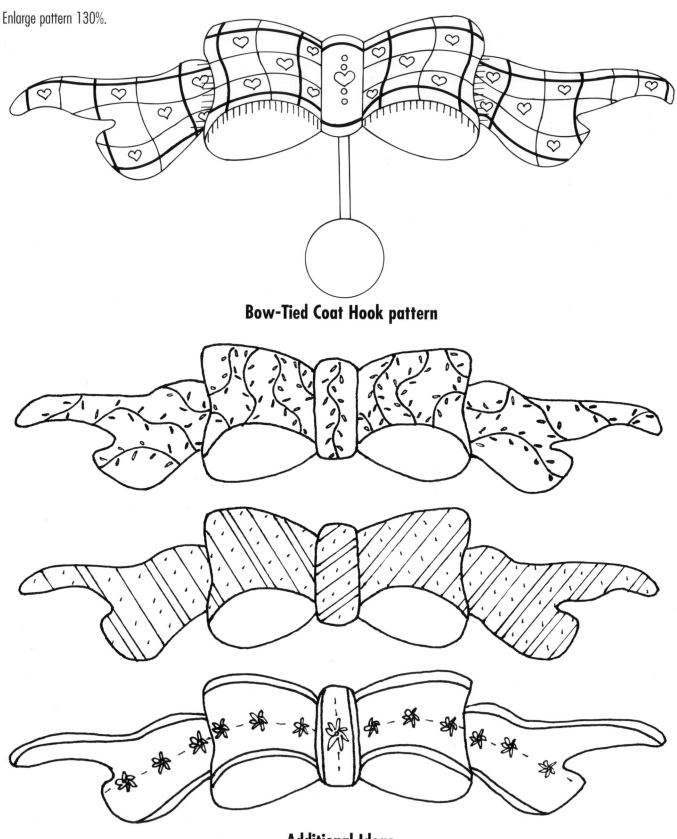

Bow-Tied Coat Hook pattern

Additional Ideas

Metric Equivalency Chart
mm-Millimeters cm-Centimeters
inches to millimeters and centimeters

inches	mm	cm	inches	cm	inches	cm
⅛	3	0.3	9	22.9	30	76.2
¼	6	0.6	10	25.4	31	78.7
½	13	1.3	12	30.5	33	83.8
⅝	16	1.6	13	33.0	34	86.4
¾	19	1.9	14	35.6	35	88.9
⅞	22	2.2	15	38.1	36	91.4
1	25	2.5	16	40.6	37	94.0
1¼	32	3.2	17	43.2	38	96.5
1½	38	3.8	18	45.7	39	99.1
1¾	44	4.4	19	48.3	40	101.6
2	51	5.1	20	50.8	41	104.1
2½	64	6.4	21	53.3	42	106.7
3	76	7.6	22	55.9	43	109.2
3½	89	8.9	23	58.4	44	111.8
4	102	10.2	24	61.0	45	114.3
4½	114	11.4	25	63.5	46	116.8
5	127	12.7	26	66.0	47	119.4
6	152	15.2	27	68.6	48	121.9
7	178	17.8	28	71.1	49	124.5
8	203	20.3	29	73.7	50	127.0

yards to meters

yards	meters	yards	meters	yards	meters	yards	meters	yards	meters
⅛	0.11	2⅛	1.94	4⅛	3.77	6⅛	5.60	8⅛	7.43
¼	0.23	2¼	2.06	4¼	3.89	6¼	5.72	8¼	7.54
⅜	0.34	2⅜	2.17	4⅜	4.00	6⅜	5.83	8⅜	7.66
½	0.46	2½	2.29	4½	4.11	6½	5.94	8½	7.77
⅝	0.57	2⅝	2.40	4⅝	4.23	6⅝	6.06	8⅝	7.89
¾	0.69	2¾	2.51	4¾	4.34	6¾	6.17	8¾	8.00
⅞	0.80	2⅞	2.63	4⅞	4.46	6⅞	6.29	8⅞	8.12
1	0.91	3	2.74	5	4.57	7	6.40	9	8.23
1⅛	1.03	3⅛	2.86	5⅛	4.69	7⅛	6.52	9⅛	8.34
1¼	1.14	3¼	2.97	5¼	4.80	7¼	6.63	9¼	8.46
1⅜	1.26	3⅜	3.09	5⅜	4.91	7⅜	6.74	9⅜	8.57
1½	1.37	3½	3.20	5½	5.03	7½	6.86	9½	8.69
1⅝	1.49	3⅝	3.31	5⅝	5.14	7⅝	6.97	9⅝	8.80
1¾	1.60	3¾	3.43	5¾	5.26	7¾	7.09	9¾	8.92
1⅞	1.71	3⅞	3.54	5⅞	5.37	7⅞	7.20	9⅞	9.03
2	1.83	4	3.66	6	5.49	8	7.32	10	9.14

index